Diarmuid Brittain

CCEA | GCSE

FRENCH VOCABULARY BOOK 2

Local, National, International & Global Areas of Interest

COLOURPOINT
EDUCATIONAL

© Diarmuid Brittain and Colourpoint Creative Ltd 2022

ISBN: 978 1 78073 287 9

First Edition
First impression

Layout and design: April Sky Design
Printed by: GPS Colour Graphics Ltd, Belfast

The Author

Diarmuid Brittain taught French for 26 years at Grosvenor Grammar School, Belfast. He is also an A level French Examiner for an awarding body.

He lives with his wife and three children in Belfast and remains a Francophile through and through.

This book has borrowed inspiration from hundreds of pupils over the years and it is dedicated to each and every language student and teacher that has graced the doors of Grosvenor Grammar School.

COLOURPOINT
EDUCATIONAL

Colourpoint Educational
An imprint of Colourpoint Creative Ltd
Colourpoint House
Jubilee Business Park
21 Jubilee Road
Newtownards
County Down
Northern Ireland
BT23 4YH

Tel: 028 9182 0505
E-mail: sales@colourpoint.co.uk
Website: www.colourpoint.co.uk

This book has been written to help students preparing for the GCSE French specification from CCEA. While Colourpoint Educational and the author have taken every care in its production, we are not able to guarantee that the book is completely error-free. Additionally, while the book has been written to closely match the CCEA specification, it is the responsibility of each candidate to satisfy themselves that they have fully met the requirements of the CCEA specification prior to sitting an exam set by that body. For this reason, and because specifications change with time, we strongly advise every candidate to avail of a qualified teacher and to check the contents of the most recent specification for themselves prior to the exam. Colourpoint Educational therefore cannot be held responsible for any errors or omissions in this book or any consequences thereof.

Contents

Introduction

This is one of four books that form a resource for English-speaking students of French and which seeks to promote **student-led vocabulary acquisition**. It is designed to **promote independent learning** and **free up teacher time**. While it is tailored for GCSE students, it is a powerful resource for all English-speaking students of French.

What do the books cover?

Various GCSE French syllabi (CCEA, WJEC, Edexcel, AQA, OCR) have common vocabulary lists. While this resource makes specific reference to the CCEA specification, it covers the vocabulary listed in all these syllabi and can be used with all of them.

The resource is divided into four books, the first three of which cover the three areas of core vocabulary as presented in the GCSE syllabi:
1. Identity, Lifestyle and Culture
2. Local, National, International and Global Areas of Interest (this book)
3. School Life, Studies and the World of Work

The resource is completed by a fourth book:
4. Verbs, Conjunctions and Other Useful Phrases, which includes an alphabetical list of the most common verbs in French, as well as a list of common connectors, *la Colle Française* (French glue).

Why these books?

- These books are designed to be used independently by students.
- Traditionally, students have been given lists of vocabulary to learn without pronunciation guides and without *aide-mémoires*. With these books, teachers can hand vocabulary learning over to their students, giving the teacher more time to focus on the challenging grammar that requires teacher-led pedagogy.
- Research shows that pupils prefer to learn from hard copies.
- Pupils can have a sense of ownership of this a resource because they can annotate it.
- The most recent GCSE CCEA specification (first examined in 2017) places more emphasis on Listening and Reading, demanding a higher level of vocabulary acquisition.
- This resource can be used independently by students from Year 8 onwards, building over five years to GCSE success. This is particularly useful for schools that need to use remote learning from time to time.

What is the structure of this book?

The vocabulary in the book is presented in the same order as it is presented in the CCEA GCSE syllabus, i.e. in alphabetical order by the English meaning.

Each word has a **pronunciation guide**. The benefits of this are the following:

- Learners can check their pronunciation of the word.
- Learners can test understanding from looking only at the pronunciation guide, thereby improving their listening skills.
- Learners can test themselves on how to write – in correct French – the phonetically described word, thereby improving the accuracy of their writing.
- Learners can work in pairs to test each other orally from English to French and/or French to English.

Most words also have an **aide-mémoire**. *Aide-mémoire* is French for 'memory aid'. People often struggle under the burden of learning vocabulary, and take little pleasure from the task.

It is the author's belief that if a student can find links between their own language and a foreign one, it makes the process of vocabulary acquisition more of a journey of discovery than a drudgery, and importantly, it allows the learner to hook the foreign words onto words that have already been assimilated in their brain.

The author likes to work with the premise 'words can make you laugh!' There are a number of attempts to be humorous throughout the book, in an effort to link works to the mind of the student. Learners may describe these attempts as 'dad jokes' – but the author believes that learners secretly like them!

The book also includes sections entitled **Practise!** These allow students to practise what they have learned, embedding their learning. Teachers will also find these sections useful in order to set homework or cover work.

What are the tick boxes for?

Each word has three tick boxes. These are provided in order to give the student a way to track their progress and organise their learning. The author suggests the following approach, though you can use whatever method works for you:

- Tick the first box when you have learned the word for the first time. When you are organising your revision use this tick to indicate to yourself what you have covered.
- When you come back later to check that you have retained the word, you can tick the second box.
- By the time you go in to your GCSE exams, you should have been able to tick the third box, to show that you have embedded that word in your brain.

Abbreviations

The book uses the following abbreviations:

(m)	masculine	e.g. *Un garçon*, a boy
(f)	feminine	e.g. *Une fille*, a girl
(m/f)	masculine or feminine	e.g. *Un/une professeur*, a teacher
(mpl)	masculine plural	e.g. *Des garçons*, (some) boys
(fpl)	feminine plural	e.g. *Des filles*, (some) girls

1. Les pièces dans la maison
[Rooms in the house]

Word or phrase	Pronunciation guide	Aide-mémoire	English meaning	Check
Appartement (m)	ah-paahr-teuh-maw		Apartment/flat	
Grenier (m)	greuh-nee-ay	Grainary, a higher part of the house is where grain was stored away from rats	Attic	
Chez moi	shay-mwah	Chez moi, chez toi, Chez McDo: At my place, at your place, at McDonald's.	At my place (home)	
Balcon (m)	bahl-kaw		Balcony	
Sous-sol (m)	souh-sawl	Sous – sub – under, sol – soil, ground	Basement	
Salle de bains (f)	sahl-deuh-bah	Salle, linked to salon, a room, a saloon. Bains – baths, bathe, salon of baths.	Bathroom	
Chambre (f)	shawm-breuh	'Chamber' is an old word for bedroom, 'in my lady's chamber'	Bedroom	
Chambre (f) de mon frère	shawm-breuh deuh maw frair	Chamber is bedroom ('in my lady's chamber'), Friar Tuck, Brother Tuck	Bedroom (brother's)	
Chambre (f) de mon père	shawm-breuh deuh maw pair	Chamber is bedroom ('in my lady's chamber'), paternal, pop, père	Bedroom (father's)	
Chambre (f) de ma grand-mère	shawm-breuh deuh ma graw-mair	Chamber is bedroom ('in my lady's chamber'), grand-mare, mère	Bedroom (grand-mother's)	
Chambre (f) de ma mère	shawm-breuh deuh ma mair	Chamber is bedroom ('in my lady's chamber'), Mother horse, mare, mère	Bedroom (mother's)	
Chambre (f) de mes parents	shawm-breuh deuh may pah-raw	Chamber is bedroom ('in my lady's chamber'), parents	Bedroom (parents')	
Chambre (f) de ma sœur	shawm-breuh deuh mah sir	Chamber is bedroom ('in my lady's chamber'). Sorority, sisterhood, soeur.	Bedroom (sister's)	
Cave (f)	kahv	Cavern, cave, a cool place for storage, maybe	Cellar	
Véranda (f)	vay-rawn-dah	A veranda is an open-air porch in English, close enough to a conservatory	Conservatory	
En bas	awhe-bah	A bass note is a low note	Downstairs	
Entrée (f)	awn-tray	**Entr**y point to the house	Entrance hall	
Étage (m)	ay-tah-zheuh	There are often 3 s**tages** (floors) to a house. Remember: 'é' at start replaces 's'.	Floor	
Premier étage (m)	prem-ee-air ay-tah-zheuh	Premier league is the first league. We know étage, stage, floor.	Floor (1st floor)	
Garage (m)	gaa-ra-zheuh		Garage	
Jardin (m)	daw leuh zhaarh-dah	Garden and jardin	Garden	
Rez-de-chaussée (m)	ray-deuh-show-say	**Ch**aussée is linked to causeway, pathway, ground level	Ground floor	
Maison (f)	may-zaw	Mansion	House	

Word or phrase	Pronunciation guide	Aide-mémoire	English meaning	Check
Cuisine (f)	kwee-zeen	Cuisine also means cookery, linked to 'culinary' (to do with cooking)	Kitchen	
Salon (m)	sahl-law	Saloon	Living room	
Salle (f) de séjour	sahl-deuh-say-zhouhr	Saloon. To sojourn somewhere is to holiday, relax somewhere.	Living room	
Bureau (m)	booh-roh	'Un bureau de change' is a money changing office	Office	
Terrasse (f)	tair-ass	A terrace is a patio	Patio	
Pièce (f)	lay pee-yes	A piece of a house is a room	Room	
Cabane (f)	kah-bahn	Cabin, log cabin	Shed	
Escalier (m)	ess-kah-lee-ay	An escalator is a moving flight of stairs that you climb or **scal**e	Stairs	
Les WC (mpl)	lay vay-say	Water closet	Toilet	
En haut	awhe-oh	**H** for **h**igh. A **hau**ghty person holds themselves above others.	Upstairs	
Buanderie (f)	booh-awn-deuh-ree	Launderie (laundry) done in the buanderie	Utility room	
Salle d'eau (f)	sahl-doh	**Sal**on of **aqu**a – room of water	Wet room/ shower room	

Practise!

Here are a few phrases you will need to know for this exercise:

La maison de mes rêves serait	My dream house would be
Il y aurait	There would be
Pour que mes amis puissent rester	So that my friends could stay
J'aurais	I would have
Je ferais construire	I would build (literally, I would make to be built)
J'aimerais qu'il y ait	I would like there to be

1. Translate into English:

La maison de mes rêves serait très grande. Elle serait dans le sud de la France. Elle serait à 5 minutes de la mer maximum. Dans la maison de mes rêves, il y aurait une piscine car j'adore nager mais je n'aime pas nager avec d'autres personnes. Aussi, dans la maison, il y aurait cinq chambres pour que mes amis puisssent rester avec moi. J'aimerais qu'il y ait une salle d'eau dans chaque chambre car c'est pratique. Aussi, j'aimerais qu'il y ait un grand jardin pour qu'on puisse jouer au football.

Finalement, j'aurais une très grande cuisine car tout le monde aime bavarder dans la cuisine et aussi, j'aurais un énorme salon, comme un cinéma pour pouvoir regarder mes films préférés.

_____

_____

_____

_____

_____

_____

2. Now try to use the vocabulary above to describe your dream house:

_____

_____

_____

_____

_____

2: Le jardin
(The garden)   *(Not on the CCEA core vocabulary list)*

Word or phrase	Pronunciation guide	Aide-mémoire	English meaning	Check
Jardin (m)	jaahr-dah	**Jardin**	Garden	
Banc (m)	baw	**Banc** linked to **benc**h	Bench	
Branche (f)	brawh-sh		Branch	
Buisson (m)	bwee-saw	Link from **bu**sh to **bui**sson	Bush	
Arbuste (m)	aarh-boost	**Arb**oretum is a tree garden, also link to **bus**h, ar**bus**te	Bush (shrub)	
Culture (f)	coohl-toohr	**Cult**ivating is linked, you grow a crop and you grow a yoghurt culture	Crop	
Fleur (f)	fleuhr		Flower	
Herbe (f)	airb	Herbs are grasses	Grass	
Serre (m)	sair	Serre, searing heat in greenhouse. Serre is like verre (glass). Glass is linked to 'vert' (green). 10 bottles (glass).	Greenhouse	
Pelouse (f)	peuh-louhze	'Pelouse don't walk on the grass!'	Lawn	
Gazon (m)	gah-zaw	Link to **gras**s	Lawn	
Tondeuse (f)	tawn-deuhze	-euse is the feminine ending because it describes la machine. Tondre – cut.	Lawnmower	
Feuille (f)	fay-yeuh	A port**folio** is a big 'leaf of paper' carrier, where 'port' is 'carry' and a folio is a leaf of paper, feuille	Leaf	
Tondre	tawn-dreuh	A monk has a hairstyle called a '**ton**sure': head is shaven on the crown, link to cut	Mow, cut	
Plante (f)	plawnt		Plant	
Racine (f)	rah-seen	Your **rac**e is where you have your roots	Root	
Bêche (f)	besh	Where do you use the spade? On the bèche! For digging in sand.	Spade	
Arbre (m)	aah-breuh	**Arb**oretum is a tree garden	Tree	
Potager (m)	poh-tah-zhay	Vegetables to go into the **pot**. Potage is sometimes used in English to denote vegetable soup.	Vegetable garden	

Practise!

1. Even though you may not feel that you are an artist, draw a garden scene on a separate sheet of paper, labelling the elements in the picture with the vocabulary above, in French.

3. Dans ma maison
[In my house]

Word or phrase	Pronunciation guide	Aide-mémoire	English meaning	Check
Climatisation (f)	klee-mat-ee zass-yaw	**Climatis**ing is what it does, it adjusts the indoor climate	Air-conditioning	
Fauteuil (m)	foh-tay	'au' is sitting between 'f' and 't' because 'eu' is il(l). Désolé, je sais que c'est nul!	Armchair	
Lavabo (m)	lah-vah-boh	**Lav** is included, which points to lavatory or laundry, which point to water. **Bo** suggests bowl, like basin, sink.	Bathroom sink	
Lit (m)	lee	The candle is lit and I'm going to bed	Bed	
Table de chevet (f)	taa-bleuh deuh sheuh-vay	What do you do with the book? Shovit (chevet) behind the bedside table!	Bedside table	
Immeuble (m)	ee-meuh-bleuh	Immeuble sounds like 'unmovable', like a block of flats. Put the two 'm's on their side, different stories, levels.	Block of flats	
Bibliothèque (f)	bee-blee-oh-tek	Bible, a book, on the bookshelf	Bookcase (library)	
Bol (m)	bawl		Bowl	
Boîte (f)	bwaaht	**Bo**x, which has the first two letters of **bo**île, is like a tin, a round tin box	Box, tin, can	
Moquette (f)	mock-ett	Rhymes with car-pet. A 'mock' floor, not real stone	Carpet	
Plafond (m)	plah-faw	'Tall Paul was fond of his ceiling'	Ceiling	
Chauffage (m) central	show-fah-zheuh sawn-traal	Chauffer means to heat. A chauffeur would heat up the car for his ladyship. As a noun, chauff**age**, like gar(er)age.	Central heating	
Commode (f)	koh-moh-deuh	The two 'm's, if turned on their side, are the drawers of a chest of drawers. The 'o's are the handles. Don't pee in this one!	Chest of drawers	
Chaise (f)	shezz	Chair	Chair	
Cafetière (f)	kaf-tee-yair	Café – coffee	Coffee-pot	
Ordinateur (m)	ore-dee-nat-euhr	Co-ordinates	Computer	
Béton (m)	bay-taw	You can 'bét on' it lasting	Concrete	
Cuisinière (f)	wee-zeen-yair	At the centre of the cuisine is the cuisinière. Cuisine means cooking or kitchen.	Cooker	
Tasse (f)	tah-seuh	The word, 'tea' is hidden in a tasse, tea-cup	Cup	
Placard (m)	plah-kaarh	**Plac**e your cup on the bo**ard**	Cupboard	
Rideaux (mpl)	ree-doh	A reed curtain. Oh!	Curtains	
Couverts (mpl)	kouh-vair	The **c u t** of cutlery (**co**u**ver**ts) is hidden in this word. Knives, forks and spoons **co**u**ver**ts the table.	Cutlery	
Lave-vaisselle (m)	lahv-vay-sell	**Lav** points to lavatory or laundry, which point to water and washing. This is a vessel (**vai**s**sel**le) for dishes.	Dishwasher	

Word or phrase	Pronunciation guide	Aide-mémoire	English
Porte (f)	port	A port to a different room	Door
Tiroir (m)	teer-wire	'-oir' is a place, and tirer is to pull. You pull or draw it out, a drawer.	Drawer
Électroménager (m)	ay-lek-troh-may-nah-zhay	Managing the house with electrical equipment	Electric apps
Plancher (m)	plaw-shay	**Planc**(k)s of wood form **her** floor.	Floor
Frigo (m)	free-goh	Frigid, cold, freezing	Fridge
Fourchette (f)	four-shett	Fourc	Fork
Meubles (mpl)	meuh-bleuh	Movable, unlike a block of flats, which is immeuble, unmovable	Furniture
Verre (m)	vair	A **verre**y handy container	Glass
Fer (m) à repasser	fair ah reuh-pass-ay	**Fer**rous oxide is iron oxide. Chemical symbol for iron is **Fe**. You pass and **re-pass** the iron over clothes.	Iron
Gazon (m)	gah-zaw	**Gaz**on bears a resemblance to grass (grass-on) on the grass.	Lawn
Pelouse (f)	peuh-louhz	Sleep on the **pillows** on the lawn	Lawn
Bouilloire (f)	bwee-wire	Boil	Kettle
Couteau (m)	couh-toe	The word '**cut**' is in this word – c**out**eau	Knife
Lampe (f)	lawm-peuh		Lamp (light)
Four à micro-ondes (m)	fouh-euhr ah mee-croh	Four rings on a cooker – what's beneath? The oven! 'Micro' helps too	Microwave oven
Micro-onde (m)	meek-roh awnd	Micro plus onde, waves **ond**ulate	Microwave oven
Serviette (f)	sair-vee-yet	A serviette is a napkin	Napkin, towel
Four (m)	fou-euhr	Four hobs above an oven. Petits fours are little warm snacks. **Four**nace.	Oven
Poêle (f)	pwaa	This is a pan, the same starting word, frying a ^ (bacon) and an l, sausage	Pan
Assiette (f)	ah-see-yet	'Ah siet' is what you might say if you drop a plate	Plate
Casserole (f)	kass-euh-role	A casserole dish is cooked in a pot	Pot
Tapis (m)	tap-ee	Tapestry is basically a rug hanging on the wall	Rug
Étagère (f)	ay-tah-zhair	'é' replaces 's' at the start of a word, stages, shelf	Shelf
Évier (m)	ay-vee-ay	'é' replaces 's' at the start of a word. Also, évian is water and you pour it down a sink.	Sink
Canapé (m)	can-ap-ay	A canopy is a cloth covering, like a hammock, which you rest on	Sofa
Divan (m)	dee-vaw	There is a sofa in da back of dee van	Sofa
Cuillère (f)	kwee-air	A spoon is a cuillère knife, pronounced (kwee-yair) – a kwee-yair, queer knife	Spoon
Table (f)	taa-bleuh		Table
Nappe (f)	nap	A napkin is a little, child version of a 'nappe'. ('Kin' means 'child', kinder, kindergarten). Small table cloth.	Table cloth

Word or phrase	Pronunciation guide	Aide-mémoire	English meaning	Check
Dessous (m) de plat	deuh-souh deuh plah	Sous – sub – under the plate	Table mat	
Théière (f)	tay-yair	Thé – tea	Teapot	
Grille-pain (m)	gree-pah	Grill-bread. 'Pain' is bread.	Toaster	
Sèche-linge (m)	sesh-lah-zheuh	Sec, dry (has got the **se** of de**se**rt). Linge, lingerie, garments.	Tumble dryer	
Armoire (f)	arm-wire	Anything with -oir(e) is a place and you can reach your whole arm in here	Wardrobe	
Lave-linge (m)	lahv-lah-zheuh	**Lav** is included, which points to lavatory or laundry, which point to water. Linge, lingerie, garments.	Washing machine	
Machine à laver (f)	mah-sheen ah lav-ay	A machine for washing. **Lav** is included, which points to lavatory or laundry, which point to water and washing.	Washing machine	

Practise!

1. Categorise the things that are listed in this section into the following groups. Write the item down in French.

Structural

1. _____
2. _____
3. _____
4. _____
5. _____
6. _____

To do with furniture

1. _____
2. _____
3. _____
4. _____
5. _____
6. _____

To do with washing

1. _____
2. _____
3. _____
4. _____
5. _____
6. _____

To do with eating / drinking

1. _____
2. _____
3. _____
4. _____
5. _____
6. _____

To do with sitting

1. _____
2. _____
3. _____
4. _____
5. _____
6. _____

Other

1. _____
2. _____
3. _____
4. _____
5. _____
6. _____

4. La salle de bains
(The bathroom) *(Not on the CCEA core vocabulary list)*

Word or phrase	Pronunciation guide	Aide-mémoire	English meaning	Check
Salle (f) de bains	saal deuh bah	Salle, linked to salon, saloon, **bains** – baths	Bathroom	
Baignoire (f)	bain-wire	'-oir' is a place, a place where the bain, **ba**th takes place	Bathtub	
Peigne (m)	pen-yeuh	No point combing your hair with a pen	Comb	
Après-shampooing (m)	ap-ray shawm-pwah	Après-ski means after skiing. Après – after, you put this in after shampoo.	Conditioner	
Déodorant (m)	day-oh-day-raw		Deodorant	
Gant (m) de toilette	gaw deuh twah-let	'Thrown down the gauntlet' means to throw glove to the ground, toilet glove	Face cloth	
Brosse (f) à cheveux	bross-ah-sheuh-veuh	Cheveux makes you think of horses with their long manes of hair	Hair brush	
Gel (m) coiffant	zhel kwah-faw	Gel to quiff your hair	Hair gel	
Crème (f) hydratante	crem ee-drat-awnt	Hydrating is 'moistening', dehydrated = dry, hydrated = moistened	Moisturiser	
Coupe-ongles (m)	coup-awn-gleuh	A coupé car is one whose roof is cut off, the a**ngle**d hard bit at end of finger	Nail clipper	
Shampooing (m)	shawm-pwah		Shampoo	
Rasoir (m)	rah-zwire	Like razor	Shaver	
Mousse (f) à raser	mousse-ah-rahz-ay	Mousse is soft fluffy stuff, to do what you do with a razor	Shaving foam	
Douche (f)	douh-sheuh	This is the sound, 'doush', as water falls on your head	Shower	
Pomme (f) de douche	pawm deuh douh-sheuh	The apple of the shower describes the shape of this part of the shower	Shower head	
Savon (m)	sah-vaw	**Sa-o** are letters that are in this as well as in **soa**p. Savlon cream is anti-septic, anti-dirt.	Soap	
Carrelage (m)	kah-reuh-lahzhe	Carré – square. A carrel is a square-shaped study area. Square hard flooring.	Tiled floor	
WC (mpl)	vay-say	**W**ater **C**loset	Toilet	
Toilettes (fpl)	twah-let		Toilet	
Papier (m) toilette	pap-yeah twah-let		Toilet paper	
Brosse (f) à dents	bross-ah-daw	Brosse, looks like brush. Dents suggests dentist.	Toothbrush	
Dentifrice (f)	dawn-tee-freese	For your dents, cool, freesing taste	Toothpaste	

Word or phrase	Pronunciation guide	Aide-mémoire	English meaning	Check
Serviette (f)	sair-vee-ett	A serviette at a table is like a mini one of these	Towel	
Lavabo (m)	lah-vah-boh	**Lava**tory is to do with water, as is a lavabo. 'bo' for 'bowl.	Wash-hand basin	

Practise!

List, in French and in English, the ten most important items in the section on the bathroom. Do not include the bathroom itself. These items should be ordered in terms of importance, with 1 the most important. Be prepared to defend your choice!

Français   Anglais

1. _____ _____

2. _____ _____

3. _____ _____

4. _____ _____

5. _____ _____

6. _____ _____

7. _____ _____

8. _____ _____

9. _____ _____

10. _____ _____

5. Les tâches ménagères
[Household jobs]

Word or phrase	Pronunciation guide	Aide-mémoire	English meaning	Check
Lit, faire le	fair leuh lee	Faire sounds like fare, how are you **far**ing, **fare**well. Lee **lit**erally lies on the bed.	Bed, to make the	
Chambre, ranger ma	raw-zhay mah shawm-breuh	Ar**range** things in my **chamber**	Bedroom, to tidy my	
Poubelles (fpl), sortir les	sore-teer lay pouh-bell	Things that **poo** and sm**ell**, poubelle. A **sorti**e, is a flight **out** in a jet fighter. **Sort i**t (take it) **out**!	Bins, to take out the	
Cuisine, faire la	fair lah kwee-zeen	Cuisine is used in English, to mean cookery. Also, same first letter, **c**ook**in**g.	Cooking, to do the	
Dîner, préparer le	pray-pah-ray leuh dee-nay		Dinner, to prepare the	
Vaisselle, faire la	fair lah vay-sell	**La**vatory, **la**undry to do with water, vaisselle – you wash the 'vessels'	Dishes, to do the	
Vaisselle, Essuyer la	ess-wee-ay lah vay-sell	Ess-wee-ay is onomatopoeic for wiping, swiping, ess-wee-ay (just say it!)	Dishes, to dry the	
Vaisselle, ranger la	raw-zhay la vay-sell	Ar**range** the vaiselle means to put it away	Dishes, to put away the	
Lave-vaisselle, vider le	vee-day leuh lahv vay-sell	Make the lave-vaiselle **v**o**id**, empty	Dishwasher, to empty the	
Lave-vaisselle, remplir le	rawm-pleer leuh lahv vay-sell	**Repl**enish is to fill up	Dishwasher, fill the	
Chien, promener le	Prom-en-ay leuh shee-yeah	Chien, **can**in**e**. A **promen**ade is a walk-way by the beach.	Dog, to walk the	
épousseter	ay-pou-sett-ay	**Pou**der is dust, **pouss**h it away	Dusting, to do the	
Jardinage, faire le	fair leuh zhar-dee-nah-zheuh	Faire sounds like fare, how are you **far**ing, **fare**well. J**ardin**age is like g**ard**en**ing.	Gardening, to do the	
Ménage, faire le	fair leuh may-nah-zheuh	How are you **far**ing, **fare**well. Ménage-à-trois, literally, household of three. Can you **m**a**nage** home?	Housework, to do the	
Repassage, faire le	fair leuh reuh-pah-sah-zheuh	Faire, like fare, how are you **far**ing, **fare**well. Pass and repass the iron over the clothes.	Ironing, to do the	
Courses, faire les	fair lay kouhrse	**Cour**iers run around doing courses in shopping	Shopping, to do the	
Table, mettre la	met-reuh lah tah bleuh	Met rhymes with set. Normally 'mettre' is 'put'. I was put with who I met. My remit – what I am put to do.	Table, to set the	
Table, débarasser la	day-bah-rass-ay lah tah-bleuh	Get rid of the **déb r i s** from the table	Table, to clear the	
Aspirateur, passer l'	pah-say lah-spee-rat-euhr	**Pass** the re**spirat**or along the ground to breathe in dust	Vacuuming, to do the	

Word or phrase	Pronunciation guide	Aide-mémoire	English meaning	Check
Lessive, faire la	fair lah less-eeve	The more washing you do, the '**lessive**' it you have to do	Washing, to do the	
Linge, faire le	fair leuh lah-zheuh	Lingerie, light clothing, clothing, clothes, do the clothes, wash them	Washing, to do the	
Fenêtres, nettoyer les	net-wy-yay lay feuh-net-reuh	Cl**ean** your **net** curtains which hang on the window which looks out on the **fen**c**e**	Windows, to clean the	

Practise!

1. Choose nine of these activities and arrange them, in French, in the order that you have done them, from the one you have done the most to the one that you have done the least.

    1. _____

    2. _____

    3. _____

    4. _____

    5. _____

    6. _____

    7. _____

    8. _____

    9. _____

2. To which household task am I referring?

    A. Je dois pousser la machine par terre (on the floor) pour aspirer les petites particules de saleté.

       (saleté = dirtiness): _____

    B. Quand j'ai fini de manger, je prends toutes les choses de la table pour les mettre dans les placards et

       les tiroirs: _____

    C. Quand mon animal doit faire de l'exercise, je dois aller avec lui.

       Il adore ça: _____

6: Mon village, ma ville et ma région
[My village, my town and my region]

Word or phrase	Pronunciation guide	Aide-mémoire	English meaning	Check
Urgences (fpl)	oohr-zhawnse	In the place where **urgen**t cases go	A&E	
Publicités (fpl)	poo-blee-see-tay	Make **public**ly aware	Advertising	
Animaux (mpl)	ahn-ee-moh	-aux shows it's a plural. **Anim** looks very similar.	Animals (pets)	
Appartement (m)	ah-part-euh-maw		Apartment	
Boulangerie (f)	bouh-law-zhair-ee	A boule (ball) of dough is used to make bread. '-erie' denotes a shop, like -ery.	Bakery	
Banque (f)	bonk		Bank	
Bar (m)	baahr		Bar	
Plage (f)	plah-zheuh	Paris-plage is a false b**ea**ch constructed in Paris. A plage for all ages.	Beach	
Bord (m) de la mer	bore deuh lah mair	**Bord** points to border, edge, side. (de la – of the) **mer**maids, girls from the sea.	Beside the sea	
Poubelles (fpl)	pouh-bell	The bin **pou**hs (poos), it is **not belle**, beautiful	Bins	
Librairie (fpl)	lee-brair-ee	A false friend, although it does help because libraries deal with books too	Bookshop	
Pont (m)	paw	A pontoon is a bridge	Bridge	
Bâtiment (m)	bah-tee-maw	The battlement, part of castle **buildi**ng. The last **basti**on (â>'s') is the last refuge, building.	Building	
Bureau (m) de change	booh-roh deuh shaw-zheuh	We use this term in English	Bureau de change	
Couloir (m) de bus	couhl-wire deuh boohss	A **co**ulis is a sweet sauce which flows. People flow in a **co**rri**dor** or lane.	Bus lane	
Gare (f) routière	gaahr rouh-tee-air	A **gara**ge for vehicles that go on the road (or **rout**e)	Bus station	
Boucherie (f)	bouh-shair-ee	Looks like butchery. Also, it sells produce for the mouth (la bouche).	Butchery	
Café (m)	kah-fay		Café	
Pâtisserie (f)	pah-tee-sair-ee	â denotes an 's' after the 'a', therefore, pastry. '-erie', denoting shop.	Cake shop	
Pharmacie (f)	faahr-mah-see		Chemist	
Château (m)	shah-toh	**Ca**st**le**. The â tells us that the next letter after the circumflex is an 's'.	Castle	
Église (f)	ay-gleez	**Ec**c**lesi**astical means to do with the church	Church	
Cinéma (m)	see-nay-mah		Cinema	
Ville (f)	veel	Ville, like village **but** it is a false friend because it means town or city	City	
Hôtel (m) de ville	oh-tell deuh veal	The hostel of the town. ô tells us that the letter after the circumflex would be an 's'.	City hall	
Magasin (m) de vêtements	mag-ah-zah deuh vet-maw	**Ma**ga**sin** – shop, linked to 'monger', iron, fish **m**o**ng**er, shop keeper. ê means s, so vest.	Clothes shop	

Word or phrase	Pronunciation guide	Aide-mémoire	English meaning	Check
Ville (f) commerciale	veel kom-air-see-yaahl	Ville, like village **but** it is a false friend because it means town or city	Commercial town	
Coin (m)	kwah	Similar letters – **cor**n**er**	Corner	
Campagne (f)	kawm-pan-yeuh	Same starting word for 'countryside'. **Camp**ing takes place in the countryside.	Countryside	
Piste (f) cyclable	peast see-klah-bleuh	A piste is a path that we ski down	Cycle path	
Salle (f) de danse	sahl deuh dawss	Salle is like a salon, which is a room, room of dance	Dance hall	
Cabinet (m) dentaire	kah-bee-nay dawn-tair	The cabinet is the government main room, here, the dentist's main room	Dental surgery	
Grand magasin(m)	graw mag-ah-zah	**M**a**ga**s**in** – shop, like '**m**o**ng**er', iron, fish **m**o**ng**er, shopkeeper. Grand – big, dept store.	Department store	
Maison (f) individuelle	may-zaw ahn-dee-vee-doo-el	Maison points to **ma**n**sion**, which points to house	Detached house	
Cabinet (m) médical	kah-bee-nay may-dee-kahl	The doctor's important room is his **cabin**et	Doctor's surgery	
En ville	awe veel	Ville, like village **but** a false friend because it means town or city. En ville – in town.	Downtown	
Distractions (fpl)	deese-trak-see-yaw	They distract you from work and entertain you	Entertainment	
Ferme (f)	fair-meuh	Similar letters **f**a**rm**	Farm	
Champ (m)	shaw	Cows **ch**o**mp** grass in fields. We **camp** in fields.	Field	
Station-service (f)	stah-see-awe sair-veese	A station for servicing one's car with petrol	Filling station	
Poissonnerie (f)	pwah-sawn-air-ee	Poisson, pisces (fish zodiac sign). Poseidon – god of sea. -**erie** is the ending denoting a shop.	Fish shop	
Fleurs (fpl)	fleuhrr		Flowers	
Forêt (f)	foe-ray	'ê' tells us that the next letter is an 's'	Forest	
Fontaine (f)	fawn-ten		Fountain	
Épicerie (f)	ay-pee-sair-ee	É replaces 's', spice shop, initially what grocers dealt in.	Grocery shop	
Coiffeur (m)/ coiffeuse (f)	kwah-feuhr/ kwah-feuhzz	A qu**iff**er of hair is a dresser of hair	Hairdresser	
Salon (m) de coiffure	sah-law deuh kwah-foohr	A saloon for quiffing, fixing hair	Hairdressing salon	
Quincaillerie (f)	kahn-kye-air-ee	Sound, 'kahn, kye' the first two syllables, sound like iron clanging, metal, hardware	Hardware store	
TGV (m)	tay-zhay-vay	**T**rain à **G**rande **V**itesse. Vite – fast, linked to velocity, speed.	High-speed train	
Ville (f) historique	veel ee-stor-eek	Ville, like village **but** it is a false friend because it means town or city, historical	Historical town	
Hôpital (m)	oh-pee-tahl	ô denotes 's' after the circumflex, ho**s**pital	Hospital	
Hôtel (m)	oh-tell		Hotel	
Maison (f)	may-zaw	Maison points to **ma**n**sion**, and then to house	House	
Hypermarché (m)	ee-pair-mar-shay	Hyper is bigger than super	Hypermarket	

Word or phrase	Pronunciation guide	Aide-mémoire	English meaning	Check
Ville (f) industrielle	veel ahn-doo-stree-el	Ville, like village **but** it is a false friend because it means town or city, industrial	Industrial town	
Lac (m)	lak		Lake	
Centre (m) de loisirs	sawn-treuh deuh lwah-zear	Centre of **leis**u**re**s	Leisure centre	
Centre (m) sportif	sawn-treuh spore-teef		Leisure centre	
Bibliothèque (f)	bee-blee-oh-tek	Bible, a book, a -thèque is a building, like discothèque. A book building.	Library	
Feu (m) feux (mpl)	feuh	**Fi**r**e**, a linked four letter word, brings light and was the first light people had	Lights (traffic)	
Marché (m)	maahr-shay		Market	
Montagnes (fpl)	mawn-tan-yeuh		Mountains	
Musée (m)	moo-zay	Be a**muse**d in the **muse**um	Museum	
Bruyant (e)	brwee-yaw	**B**oist**er**ous, **br**o**uha**ha are linkable and suggest noise	Noisy	
RER (m)	air-euh-air	**Re**gional **R**ail	Paris/suburbs train	
Parc (m)	paark		Park	
Bureau (m) des passeports	booh-roh deuh pass-poahr	Bureau, as in bureaucracy, is a term which means office	Passport office	
Zone (f) piétonne	zone pee-ay-tone	**Pié**ton, **ped**estrian, **ped** is foot, **pod**iatry, foot care, zone, area	Pedestrian area	
Transports (mpl) publics	traw-spore pooh-bleek		Public transport	
Calme	kahl-meuh		Quiet, calm	
Poubelle (f) de recyclage	pouh-bell deuh reuh-see-kla-zheuh	Things that **poo** and sm**ell**, poubelle. Recycler, becomes a noun, -age, recycle-age.	Recycling bin	
Restaurant (m)	rest-oh-raw		Restaurant	
Rivière (f)	ree-vee-air		River	
Panneau (m) de route	pah-noh deuh route	A b**anne**r is rather similar. It displays advice too. A route is a road.	Road sign	
Rond-point (m)	raw-pwah	A roundabout goes a**round** about a certain **point**	Roundabout	
Mer (f)	mair	A lady who is half fish is a maid of the sea, la **mer**	Sea	
Magasin (m)	mah-gah-zah	**Ma**ga**sin** – shop, linked to 'monger', iron, fish **mong**er, shop keeper	Shop, store	
Boutique (f)	bouh-teek	A boutique is used in English to mean a shop	Shop, store	
Centre (m) commercial	sawn-treuh kom-air-see-al		Shopping centre	
Patinoire (f)	pah-teen-wire	'oir', a place, like trottoir, footpath, abattoir. P**at**in – sc**at**e, **p**u**tt**in**g** a foot on ice.	Skating rink	
Place (f)	plass	The place in the middle of the town is the square	Square (main square)	

Word or phrase	Pronunciation guide	Aide-mémoire	English meaning	Check
Rue (f)	roo	Linked to **rou**t**e**	Street	
Lampadaires (mpl)	lawmp-ah-dare	A **lamp** that **dare**s to be in the street	Street lights	
Banlieue (f)	bawl-yeuh	Lieu – place, 'in **lieu** of' means 'in place of'. **Ban**ned to a place outside the city.	Suburb outside city	
Métro (m)	may-troh	The **métro**politan underground railway runs beneath the **metro**polis	Subway, tube	
Supermarché (m)	soo-pair-mar-shay		Supermarket	
Confiserie (f)	kaw-fee-zair-ee	Confectionery, sweets	Sweet shop	
Piscine (f)	pee-seen	Some children can be caught doing this (pee-seen) in it!	Swimming pool	
Théâtre (m)	tay-at-reuh		Theatre	
Tabac-presse (m)	tah-bah press	Tabac like tobacco. Presse like the press which prints newspapers.	Tobacconist, Newsagent	
Office (m) de tourisme	oh-feese deuh touh-reeze-meuh		Tourist Office	
Syndicat (m) d'Initiative	sah-dee-kah dee-nee-see-ah-teeve	Syndicate, a group (of tourist offices in a country) which seek to help you use initiative	Tourist Office	
Ville (f) touristique	veel tour-east-eek		Tourist town	
Magasin (m) de jouets	may-zaw deuh jouh-ay	**M**aga**sin** – shop, linked to '**m**on**g**er'. Jouet, linked to jouer, to play. Toys are playthings.	Toy shop	
Ville (f)	veel	Ville, village, town, city	Town	
Circulation (f)	seer-kooh-lass-yaw	Traffic goes round and round, **circulati**ing like blood in a body	Traffic	
Embouteillage (f)	awm-bouh-tay-ah-zheuh	We refer to bottle-necks. Em**bou**t**eill**age means **bottli**ng, so that cars are stuck.	Traffic jam	
Bouchon (m)	bouh-shaw	Bouchon – cork. It goes in the mouth (bouche) of the bottle and cars are stuck.	Traffic jam	
Feux (mpl)	feuh	Feu – fire, fire is light, the lights	Traffic lights	
Gare (f)	gaar	Park your car in **gar**age, your train in **gare**	Train station	
Arbre (m)	aahr-breuh	An **arb**o**re**tum is a tree garden. These were fashionable 150 years ago.	Tree	
Couloir (m) pour camion	kouhl-wire pohr kah-mee-aw	Lane or **co**rridor for a **ca**rgo vehicle, a **ca**mion, to flow along	Truck lane	
Métro (m)	may-troh	Metropolitan service (underground in a city, a metropolis)	Underground	
Vélodrome (m)	vay-loh-drome	Vélo – a bike	Velodrome, cycling hall	
Animé(e)	aah-nee-may	If something is **anim**at**e**d it is brought to life and is vibrant	Vibrant	
Villa (m)	vee-lah		Villa	
Passage (m) piéton	pass-ah-zheuh pee-ay-taw	Pié points to pied, which points to pedestrian, paw, podiatrist, foot. Walk across.	Zebra crossing	

Practise!

1. Fill up the blanks below with French and English shops and buildings (*magasins et bâtiments*).

Français

Anglais

_____   _____

_____   _____

_____   _____

_____   _____

_____   _____

_____   _____

_____   _____

_____   _____

_____   _____

_____   _____

_____   _____

_____   _____

_____   _____

_____   _____

_____   _____

_____   _____

_____   _____

2. Fill up the blanks below with other useful words which aren't shops or buildings, i.e. others (*autres*).

Français

Anglais

_____   _____

_____   _____

_____   _____

_____   _____

_____   _____

_____   _____

_____   _____

_____   _____

_____   _____

_____   _____

_____   _____

_____   _____

_____   _____

_____   _____

_____   _____

7. Les directions
[Directions]

Word or phrase	Pronunciation guide	Aide-mémoire	English meaning	Check
Toutes directions (fpl)	touht dee-reks-yaw	**Tot**al, all of the directions	All directions	
Par ici	paahr ee-see	'Per cent' means 'of one hundred'. 'Par ici' means 'of here', which means 'around here'.	Around here	
Par là	paahr lah	Per cent' means 'of one hundred'. 'Par là' means 'of there', which means 'around there'.	Around there	
Derrière	dair-ee-air	One's derrière is one's behind, or bottom. At der**rear**, behind you.	Behind	
À côté de	ah koh-tay-deuh	ô denotes 's' after ^. To acco**st** someone means to go be**side** that person. The coast is the sea-**side**.	Beside, next to	
Centre (m)	sawn-treuh		Centre	
Continuez jusqu'aux feux	caw-tee-noo-ay zhoo-skoh feuh	**Jus**t to the lights, no further. Feux linked to **fire**.	Continue to the lights	
Traversez la place	trah-vair-say lah plass	Traversing in skiing or hill-walking is 'to cross'. The **pla**za is the town square.	Cross the square	
Directions (fpl)	dee-reks-yaw		Directions	
Est (m)	esst	**East** looks like est	East	
Partout	paahr-touh	'Par tout' means 'of all' (places). Totality of the places. Everywhere.	Everywhere	
Loin de	lwaah deuh	Rwanda (Lwaah deuh) is far from here.	Far	
Descendez la pente	dess-awnd-ay lah pawnt	Descend is go down. **Pent** up (up and down slope) emotions, **pent**house, at **the top** of the building .	Go down the slope	
Passez le pont	pah-say leuh paw	**Pass** over is go across. A **pont**oon is a bridge.	Go over the bridge	
Passez le rondpoint	pah-say leuh raw-pwah	Roundpoint, **point** that traffic goes a**round**, pass over it	Go over the roundabout	
Contournez le lac	caw-tour-nay leuh lak	**Tourner**, turn, turn around, go around	Go round the lake	
Allez tout droit	all-ay touh drwah	Go down an **alle**y, **tot**ally st**rai**ght (adroit)	Go straight ahead	
Montez la pente	mawn-tay la coat	Go up a **mo**un**t**ain. **Pent** up (up and down slope) emotions. **Pent**house, at **the top** of the building.	Go up the slope	
Ici	ee-see	Say this five times : 'Easy to be ici, Easy to be here!'	Here	
Devant	deuh-vaw	In fro**nt**. At the **van**guard is at the fro**nt**.	In front of	

Word or phrase	Pronunciation guide	Aide-mémoire	English meaning	Check
Près de	pray-deuh	**Pre**ceding something is right in front of, or beside, near to something	Near	
La prochaine rue	praw-shen	Approach means to come **next** to something, **proch**aine, rue, **rou**te	Next street	
Nord (m)	norrh	Looks like **nor**th	North	
à gauche	ah goh-sh	Gauche in English means 'awkward', like a right-hander using left! **Gosh** is that right!? No it's left!	On the left	
à droite	ah dr-waht	Maladroit in English means 'bad on the right', clumsy. A left-hander using right.	On the right	
De l'autre côté de	deuh lohtr koh-tay deuh	'Other', looks like 'autre'. ô denotes 's'after circumflex. To ac**cost**, to go to the **side** of. Other side.	On the other side	
En face de	awe fass deuh	**Fac**ing is opposite	Opposite	
Là-bas	lah-bah	Là is 'there' as in '**Voi**là' which means, 'See there!' Là-bas (bass) means 'there down', 'down there'.	Over there	
La deuxième rue	lah deuh-zee-em roo	Deux linked to duet, duo, even a duel where two people fight. Rue – road.	Second street	
Sud (m)	sood	Looks like **sou**th	South	
Arrêtez aux feux	ah-ret-ay oh feuh	ê denotes 's' after e, arrest, cardiac arrest, stop. Feux, fire, lights.	Stop at the lights	
Tout droit	touh dr-wah	If you are ad**roit**, you are skilled, **straight**-talking, dependable, not crooked	Straight on	
Prenez la première rue	pren-ay lah prem-ee-yair roo	Premier league, first league, rue linked to road	Take the first street	
Faites demi tour	fet deuh-mee tour	'Feat' is something done. Demi is like semi, half, a half-**tur**n means turn round.	Turn around (do a)	
Tournez à droite	touhr-nay ah dr-waht	**T**o**urn**ez looks like turn	Turn right	
Tout près	touh-pray	**Tot**ally **pre**ceding (just in front of, near)	Very near	
Ouest (m)	ouh-esst	Sounds like west when one says it	West	

Practise!

1. Translate the following directions into English:

A. Allez tout droit, allez tout droit. Arrêtez aux feux. Prenez la deuxième rue à droite. Continuez jusqu'aux feux. Descendez la pente. Passez le pont. Prenez la première rue à gauche. Vous êtes là!

_____

_____

_____

B. Contournez le lac. Passez le premier rondpoint. Montez la pente. Prenez la première rue à gauche. Allez tout droit pour 300 mètres. Traversez la place. Arrêtez en face de l'église. Vous êtes là!

_____

_____

_____

2. Translate these directions into French:

A. Go up the slope. Go over the roundabout. Take the first street on the right. Stop at the lights. Go over the bridge. Go through the square and stop opposite the school. You are there!

_____

_____

_____

B. Go over the bridge. Take the second street on the left. Take the first street on the right. Cross the square. Continue to the lights. Stop at the lights. Turn left. It is opposite the church.

_____

_____

_____

3. In the space below, draw a plan for someone to get from A to B. Include streets and buildings on the plan. Then describe it in French.

8. Les déplacements
(Getting around)

Word or phrase	Pronunciation guide	Aide-mémoire	English meaning	Check
Aéroport (m)	ah-ay-roh-pohr	**Aéro**port	Airport	
Arrêt (m) de bus	ah-ray deuh boose	ê denotes an 's' after the ê. Arrest means to stop, a bus stop.	Bus stop	
à vélo (m)	ah vay-loh	Velodrome, cycling arena	By bike	
En bateau (m)	awe bat-oh	Battre – to beat, the water – eau. Waves and vowels (eau) in the water.	By boat	
En bus (m)	awe boo-ss	Sounds like 'goose' but has a 'b'	By bus	
En autobus (m)	awn oh-toe-boo-ss		By bus	
En voiture (f)	awe vwah-toor	Go for a '**tour**' in your voi**tur**e, also, **Vo**lkswagen	By car	
En car (m)	awe caar	A big car is a coach	By coach	
En hélicoptère (m)	awn ay-lee-kop-tair		By helicopter	
à cheval (m)	ah sheuh-vaal	Chivalry, the behaviour associated with knights, who ride horses	By horse	
En aéroglisseur (m)	awn ah-ay-roh-glee-sir	Glisser – to slide on. Aéro – air. To slide on air.	By hovercraft	
à moto	ah moh-toh	First half of **moto**rbike	By motorbike	
En avion (m)	awn ah-vee-yaw	Aviation industry	By plane	
En fusée (f)	awe foo-zay	Light a fuse to launch the rocket	By rocket	
En taxi (m)	awe taks-ee		By taxi	
En train (m)	awe trah		By train	
Parking (m)	paarh-king		Car park	
Traversée (f)	trah-vair-say	To **traverse** is to go across, often in mountaineering. Here a boat crossing.	Crossing	
Retard (m)	reuh-taarh	If development has been **retard**ed, it has been delayed, held back.	Delay	
Automobiliste (m)	oh-toh-moh-bee-leest	An automobile is a vehicle	Driver (of a car)	
Station-service (f)	stah-see-yaw sair-veese	A **station** where one **serve**s one's car with petrol	Filling station	
Vol (m)	vall	A vol-au-vent is a light (**flighty**) pastry. A volley is an **air**-shot.	Flight	
Trajet (m)	tra-zhay	The **traje**ctory of an object is the path it follows, its journey	Journey	
à pied (m)	ah pee-yay	Pedestrian	On foot	
Carte (f)	kaart	A **cart**ographer is a map-maker	Map	
Autoroute (f)	oh-toh-rouht	Auto, like an automobile. Route, like a road, a road for motors, motorway.	Motorway	

Word or phrase	Pronunciation guide	Aide-mémoire	English meaning	Check
Passager, passagère	pah-sah-zhay, pah-sah-zhair		Passenger	
Piéton, piétonne	pee-ay-taw, pee-ay-tawn	**P**ié is linked to foot, **ped**es**tria<u>n</u>**, someone who goes by foot	Pedestrian	
Les transports (mpl) publics	lay traw-spore poo-bleek		Public transport	
GPS (m)	zhay pay ess	Global Positioning System or Géo-localisation Par Satellite	Satnav	
Péage (m)	pay-ah-zheuh	Garer – to park, gar**age**. Payer – to pay. Together gives pé**age**, the place you pay.	Toll booth (paying station)	
Tramway (m)	tram-way	The tram way, the way of the tram	Tram	
Voyageur (m)	vwy-ah-zheur	A voyager is a traveller	Traveller	
Voyage (m)	vwy-ah-zheuh	A voyage is a trip	Trip	
Métro (m)	may-troh	You get **metro**politan underground train networks in the **metro**polis	Underground train	

Practise!

Read the following descriptions and indicate what they are describing.
Answer in French and then English.

1. This is a place where you must hand in money in order to have the right to use the road:

Français _____ Anglais _____

2. This is what you have had to incur if you get caught in a traffic jam and don't get there in time:

Français _____ Anglais _____

3. If your destination was the moon, this would be the most appropriate means of transport:

Français _____ Anglais _____

4. Dark, but at least there are no traffic jams:

Français _____ Anglais _____

5. These often last longer than the journey in an airplane, but at least you can bring your car:

Français _____ Anglais _____

6. These are used to increase speed of travel and, interestingly, they are less dangerous than ordinary roads:

Français _____ Anglais _____

7. Belfast used to have these throughout the city but now their tracks are covered in tarmac:

Français _____ Anglais _____

8. The name for this mode of transport is a combination of striking and liquid:

Français _____ Anglais _____

9. Currently, these can be purchased for not that much money but they are harming the environment:

Français _____ Anglais _____

10. Sometimes, although it is useful, we can put too much trust in it and end up well and truly lost:

Français _____ Anglais _____

11. Quand le GPS n'existait pas, on utilisait ces choses pour savoir quelle route on devait prendre:

Français _____ Anglais _____

12. Quand on veut partir en avion, on doit aller ici:

Français _____ Anglais _____

13. Ce mode de transport devient de nouveau plus populaire car c'est relativement bien pour l'environnement:

Français _____ Anglais _____

14. Normalement, quand on veut prendre l'autobus, on doit attendre ici:

Français _____ Anglais _____

15. Quand il n'y avait pas de transports motorisés, on devait se déplacer en utilisant cet animal:

Français _____ Anglais _____

16. Ce sont les gens qui utilisent leurs pieds pour se déplacer:

Français _____ Anglais _____

17. C'est normalement plus grand qu'un bus, ça utilise les routes et c'est souvent pour les touristes:

Français _____ Anglais _____

18. Quand on voyage en voiture, c'est pratique mais souvent on doit trop payer pour se garer dans le......:

Français _____ Anglais _____

19. Quand on a une voiture, on doit utiliser ces endroits pour acheter de l'essence:

Français _____ Anglais _____

20. C'est un mode de transport qui est souvent utilisé pour deux personnes et c'est assez dangereux:

Français _____ Anglais _____

9: En voiture et en train
(By car and by train)

Word or phrase	Pronunciation guide	Aide-mémoire	English meaning	Check
Accélérateur (m)	ak-say-lay-rat-euhr		Accelerator	
Banquette arrière (f)	bawn-kett ah-ree-air	The **ben**ch **at** **re**ar	Back seat	
Bagnole (f)	ban-yole	An old **bagn**er, banger	Car (old banger)	
Coffre (m)	kaw-freuh	A coffer is a receptacle used for storage, like a boot	Boot	
En panne (f)	awe pahn	A right **panne** in the neck	Breakdown	
Dépanneur (m)	day-pan-euhr	To reverse a verb, put 'dé' in front, **dépanner**, is to reverse the breakdown	Breakdown mechanic	
Pare-chocs (m)	paahr-shock	Para-trooper is 'against' the trooper. Here, the **pare** is used against the choc.	Bumper	
Voiture (f)	vwah-toohr	Go for a **tour** in the voi**ture**. It is a **Vo**lkswagen. **V**a **v**a **vo**om.	Car	
Capot (m)	kah-poh	A **cap** is a sort of hood or bonnet	Car bonnet/ hood	
Toit (m)	twah	A house has a **to**p **to it**, and it is called a roof	Car roof	
Coupé (m)	kouh-pay	A car that has its roof **cu**t off is a coupé, the verb, 'couper' is 'to cut'	Coupé	
Wagon-restaurant (m)	vah-gaw rest-aw-raw		Dining car	
Chauffeur (m)	show-feuhr	Chauffer – heat, (**ca**lor gas for heating). A chauffeur used to warm the car up.	Driver	
Permis de conduire (m)	pair-mee deuh cawn-dweer	To conduct the orchestra is to drive it. 'Permis' is permission, a license to drive.	Driving licence	
Première classe (f)	prem-yee-air class		First class	
Vitesses (fpl)	vee-tess	In English, we talk of a 'four-speed' gear-box, **vite**sse is speed, **ve**locity	Gears	
Monter (v) dans le train (m)	mawn-tay daw leuh trah	To **mo**unt is to get up into or on to something	Get in the train	
Boite (f) à gants	bwat-ah-gaw	Boite – box, compartment. Gant, the **ga**unt**l**et, the glove.	Glove compartment	
Frein (m) à main	frahn-ah-mah	Take off the 'F', use the **rein**s to slow the horse down, **main**, **mani**pulate, hand	Hand brake	
Clignotant (m)	kleen-yaw-taw	I'd be in**clign**ed to think you're indicating to the right!	Indicator	
Renseignements (mpl)	raw-sen-yeuh-maw	People use **sign**s to project information (ren**seign**ments), to inform	Information	
Moniteur (m)	mawn-eat-euhr	An instructor monitors	Instructor	
Monitrice (f)	mawn-eat-reese	An instructress monitors too	Instructor (female)	

Word or phrase	Pronunciation guide	Aide-mémoire	English meaning	Check
Phares (mpl)	faahr	With these, you can see **phar** into the distance.	Light (on a car)/ Lighthouse	
Bureau (m) des objets trouvés	boo-roh days awb-zhay trouh-vay	Bureau de change – money changing office, a treasure **trove** is found	Lost-property office	
Numéro (m) d'immatriculation	nooh-may-roh dee-mat-ree-koo-lass-yaw	Matriculation is enrolment, your number is enrolled and held by police	Number plate	
Siège (m) passager	see-yeah-zheuh pah-say-zhay	**Si**e̱ge, **se**at, or you could take a seat by siege!	Passenger seat	
Quai (m)	kay	The **qua**y is where the boat departs in English, where a train departs in French	Platform	
Crevaison (f)	creh-veah-zaw	A crevasse is a big hole in the earth, a **creva**ison is a big hole in a tyre	Puncture	
Voie (f)	vwah	The **vay** forward is **via** (**voie**) the rails	Rails	
Réparateur (m)	ray-pah-rat-euhr		Repairman	
Deuxième classe (f)	deuh-zee-em class		Second class	
Pneu (m) de rechange	peuh-neuh deuh reuh shaw-zheuh	**Rechange** indicates change if necessary which is what a spare tyre is for	Spare tyre	
Faire (v) la direction (f)	fair lah dee-rek-shee-yaw	If the direction of travel is made (faire) by you, you are steering	Steer	
Volant (m)	vaw-law	If you w**ant** to steer, you **vol** have to use the **volant**, **voluntarily**.	Steering wheel	
Toit ouvrant (m)	twah ouh-vraw	An **ov**e̱rture is an opening piece of music, if something is **overt**, it is open.	Sunroof	
Passer (v) son permis (m)	pass-ay saw pair-mee	A very sneaky one, to pass is not 'passer' – passer is to sit one's '**permis**sion to drive', test	Take one's driving test	
Guichet (m)	gee-shay	**G**et ea**ch** tick**et** at the guichet	Ticket counter	
Gare (f)	gaahr	A station for your car is the **gar**age	Train station	
Pneu (m)	peuh-neuh	**Pneu**matic tyres are filled with air	Tyre	
Composter (v) le billet (m)	Kawm-paw-stay	To make **compost**, save up validated tickets, cut and then bin. A billet looks like a tick**et**.	Validate the ticket	
Wagon (m)	vah-gaw		Wagon	
Pare-brise (m)	paahr-breeze	Para-trooper is 'against' the trooper, pare-brise is against the breeze	Windscreen	
Essuie-glace (m)	ess-wee-glass	Glace, the glass of a windscreen, essuie (ess-wee, ess-wee) an onomatopoeia wipe	Windscreen wiper	
Rétroviseur (m)	ray-troh-vee-zeuhr	**Retro-vis**ion, looking back	Wing mirror	

Practise!

Fill the three categories given below with words from this section.

1. Car vocabulary.

Français   Anglais

_____   _____

_____   _____

_____   _____

_____   _____

_____   _____

_____   _____

_____   _____

_____   _____

_____   _____

_____   _____

2. Train vocabulary.

_____   _____

_____   _____

_____   _____

_____   _____

_____   _____

_____   _____

_____   _____

_____   _____

_____   _____

_____   _____

3. Applicable to either.

_____   _____

_____   _____

_____   _____

_____   _____

_____   _____

_____   _____

_____   _____

_____   _____

_____   _____

_____   _____

10: La météo
[The weather]

Word or phrase	Pronunciation guide	Aide-mémoire	English meaning	Check
Automne (m)	oh-tawn		Autumn	
Mauvais, il fait	eel fay moh-vay	**Ma**lificent is bad, mal-practice is bad	Bad	
Aléatoire	ah-lay-ah-twaahr	4 syllables in this phrase, very changeable. Will Al eat wire? It will change his stomach!	Changeable	
Climat (m)	klee-mah		Climate	
Nuageux	noo-ah-zheuh	Cumulus **n**imb**u**s, a type of cloud, 'n**eb**ul**ou**s' means clouded, unclear	Cloudy	
Nuages (mpl), il y a des	eel-ee-ah day nooh-ah-zheuh	Cumulus **n**imb**u**s, a type of cloud, 'n**eb**ul**ou**s' means clouded, unclear	Clouds, there are	
Froid, il fait	frwah	**Fr**idge, refrigerate	Cold	
Rosée (f)	roh-zay	Temperature **rose** and then fell, creating **rosée**. Dew is beautiful on a **rose**. It looks **ros**i**e**.	Dew	
Sécheresse (f)	say-shair-ess	Le vin sec – dry wine. Sécher**ess** in the wildern**ess**.	Drought	
Sec (sèche), il fait sec	sek, sesh, eel fay sek	Le vin sec – dry wine. If you are feeling sick (sec) you have a dry mouth.	Dry, it is	
Brouillard (m), il fait du	brwee-yaarh	Em**broil**ed in something is mixed up in something, can't see where to go	Foggy, it is	
Givre (m)	zheev-reuh	**Givre** (giver, give her) a scraper to scrape off the frost!	Frost	
Grêle (f), il y a de la	deuh lah grel	A big hailstone could be like a 'grêle-pan' falling on your head	Hail	
Chaleur (f)	shah-leurrh	A chauffeur warms up the seat for his boss' bottom, from chauffer. Chauffer gives chaleur.	Heat	
Canicule (f)	can-ee-cool	Canned heat, not cool	Heat-wave	
Chaud, il fait	eel fay shoh	Calor gas brings heat, a chauffeur warms up the seat for his boss' bottom. Verb: chauffer.	Hot	
Lourd, il fait	louhr	A Lord is important, a heavyweight in society, heavy weather, oppressive	Humid	
Ouragan (m), il y a un	eel-ee-ah ahn ouh-raa-gaw	Sounds like a hurricane	Hurricane, there is a	
Glace (f)	glass	Ice looks like glass and also breaks like glass	Ice	
Éclair (m)	ay-klair	Lightning is **cl**e**ar** against the dark sky	Lightning	
Température basse (f)	tawm-pay-rat-oor bass	Bass, low sound, at the base, at the bottom	Low temperature	
Doux, il fait	douh	Doudou is the French for a soft cuddly toy. **Du**lcet tones are soft tones, soft, mild.	Mild	
Brume (f)	broom	Cars, broom broom, produce a sort of mist from their exhaust pipes	Mist	
Beau, il fait	eel fay boh	Beau – first half of beautiful	Nice	

Word or phrase	Pronunciation guide	Aide-mémoire	English meaning	Check
Couvert	kouh-vair	Couvert means **cover**ed. If the sky is covered it is overcast.	Overcast	
Arc-en-ciel (m)	ark-aw-see-yell	Arch in the sky	Rainbow	
Pluie (f)	ploo-wee	Pleut pleut pleut like raindrops, pleurisy is water on the lung, pleurs are sobs	Rain (n)	
Pleut, il	eel pleuh	Pleut pleut pleut like raindrops, pleurisy is water on the lung, pleurs are sobs	Raining, it's raining	
Pluvieux	ploo-vee-yeuh	Pleut pleut pleut like raindrops, pleurisy is water on the lung, pleurs are sobs	Rainy	
Ombre (f)	awm-breuh	You will find shade under my **umbre**lla or my s**ombre**ro. It's dark and s**ombre** there.	Shadow/shade	
Averses (fpl), il y a des	days ah-vairse	**A**d**verse** conditions can be wet, not good weather conditions	Showers, there are	
Ciel (m)	see-yell	One looks up to see that there is no **ceil**ing. At least, the sky is the **ceil**ing.	Sky	
Neige, il	eel neh-zheuh	The Sneige in winter nestles in the nooks and crevices. Sn**eig**e for a sl**eig**h.	Snow	
Printemps (m)	prahn-taw	Temps means weather or time. As in, 'tempus fugit' time flies. S**prin**g is like spring, springtime.	Spring(time)	
Orage (m), il y a un	eel-ee-ah ahn oar-ah-zheuh	A **rage**ing storm	Storm, there is a	
Tempête (f), il y a une	eel-ee-ah oon tawm-pett	A tempest, a tempestuous encounter is a stormy one	Storm, there is a	
Été (m)	ay-tay	'é' at start denotes 's'. Été gives 'estival' meaning 'summery'. It is in summer that we have **F**estival**s**.	Summer	
Soleil, il fait du	eel fay doo soh-lay	Solar panel	Sunny	
Ensoleillé(e)	awe-soh-lay-yay	**Sol**ar power is sun power, ensoleillé means sunny	Sunny	
Eclaircies (fpl), il y a des	days ay-clair-see	Clear, clair spells are when the sun comes out	Sunny spells, there are	
Tonnerre (m)	tawn-air	**Tonner**re looks like thunder. Tonnerre and thunder are onomatopoeic descriptions of thunder.	Thunder	
Temps (m)	taw	The **temp**erature goes up when the weather gets up	Weather	
Prévision (f) météo	pray-veez-yaw	Pre-vision, fore-sight, a prediction, a meteorological prediction	Weather forecast	
humide	oo-meed	Humid just means wet.	Wet	
Quel temps fait-il?	kell taw fay-teel?	Quel – kell the witch (which?), sorry witch, temps – **temp**erature (weather)	What's the weather?	
Vent, il fait du	dooh vaw	Ventilator, a vent, ventilation	Windy, it is	
Hiver (m)	ee-vair	**Hi**ver**nate, some animals hibernate in winter when they s**hiver**	Winter	

Practise!

Take a look at the weather conditions and try to classify them by seasons in Paris.

1. Le printemps

Français   Anglais

_____   _____

_____   _____

_____   _____

_____   _____

_____   _____

2. L'été

_____   _____

_____   _____

_____   _____

_____   _____

_____   _____

3. L'automne

_____   _____

_____   _____

_____   _____

_____   _____

_____   _____

4. L'hiver

_____   _____

_____   _____

_____   _____

_____   _____

_____   _____

5. Toutes les saisons

_____   _____

_____   _____

_____   _____

_____   _____

_____   _____

11: L'environnement
[The environment]

Word or phrase	Pronunciation guide	Aide-mémoire	English meaning	Check
SIDA (m)	see-dah	**S**yndrome d'**I**mmuno **D**éficience **A**cquise (Aquired Immuno-Deficiency Syndrome)	Aids	
Dioxyde de carbone (m)	dee-ox-eed deuh caar-bonn	Dioxide of carbon	Carbon dioxide	
Émissions de carbone (fpl)	ay-meese-yaw deuh caar-bonn		Carbon emissions	
CFC (m)	say-eff-say		CFC gas	
Charbon (m)	shaarh-baw	**Coa**l includes three of the letters of carbon. **Char**red, means burnt. Coal is carbon.	Coal	
Consommation (f)	kaw-saw-mass-yaw	**Cons**o**mm**a**tion**. Consuming is consumption.	Consumption	
Contamination (f)	kaw-tah-mee-nass-yaw		Contamination	
Jour (m)	jouhr	**Jour**nal, daily report, bon**jour** – good**day**	Day	
Déboisement (m)	day-bwazz-maw	The 'dé' renders negative. Le boisement, planting trees. Remember: boy(i)s like trees.	Deforestation	
Sécheresse (f)	say-shair-ess	After a drinking se**ch**ion, there is no liquid left	Drought	
Terre, terre (f)	tair	**Terr**itory, **terr**ain, both mean earth, land	Earth, earth	
Séisme (m)	say-eeze-meuh	Geologists measure 'seismic' activity	Earthquake	
Tremblement (m) de terre	trawm-bleuh-maw deuh tair	**Trembl**ing of the **terr**itory is the same as quaking of the earth, earthquake	Earthquake	
En voie de disparition (f)	awe vwah deuh dee-spah-reese-yaw	Via, a road, 'to Rome via (voie) Paris', road to disappearance, linked to **dispar**ition	Endangered species	
Environnement (m)	awe-vee-rawn-euh-maw		Environment	
Disette (f)	dee-sett	**Seventeen** (dix-sept) countries without food	Famine	
Inondations (fpl)	ee-nawn-dass-yaw	Inundated with problems means 'flooded' with	Flood	
Combustibles (fpl) fossiles	cawm-boost-ee-bleuh faw-seel	Combustible means burnable, like fuel	Fossil fuels	
Réchauffement (m) climatique	ray-showff-maw deuh lah tair	Reheating is réchauffement (chaud – hot, is in there)	Global warming	
Effet de serre (m)	ay-fay deuh sair	Effet, **effe**ct. Serre rhymes with verre, verre is glass, which can be green, vert	Greenhouse effect	
Nuisible	nwee-zee-bleuh	If something is a **nuis**an**ce** it is normally, in some way, harmful	Harmful	
Trou (m)	trouh	Both words have an O in the middle. That is the tr**o**uth, the w**hole** tr**o**uth and nothing but the tr**o**uth.	Hole	
Ordures (fpl) ménagères	oar-doohr may-nah-zhair	The binmen got their **ord**ur**es** (orders). Ménagères describes. **Man**a**ge** a household.	Household rubbish	

Word or phrase	Pronunciation guide	Aide-mémoire	English meaning	Check
Fonte de la calotte (f)	fawnt deuh lah kah-lot	A chocolate **fon**du, is melted chocolate, la **ca**lotte, ice-**cap**, a ca**lot** of ice	Ice cap melt	
Forêt tropicale (f)	fore-ay trop-ee-kahl	ê denotes 's' after the ê	Rainforest	
Lune (f)	loon	**Lun**ar cycle – cycle of the moon, **lun**atic, driven mad by the moon	Moon	
Nature (f)	naah-toohr		Nature	
Nuit (f)	nwee	**Nu**it, night, **noc**turnal	Night	
Azote (m)	ah-zoat	Azotos is the Greek for 'lifeless'. Nitrogen is a dead gas, anti-combustion.	Nitrogen	
Centrale (f) nucléaire	sawn-traal	All the energy is located in this **centre**	Nuclear Power station	
Déchets nucléaires (mpl)	day-shay noo-klay-air	When you do the (déchets) **dishes**, that stuff in the plughole is the waste	Nuclear waste	
Pétrole (m)	pay-troll	Petrol is made from oil	Oil	
Surpeuplé (e)	soohr-peuh-play	'Pe**uplé**', populated. 'Sur' is 'super'. **Sur**humain, **su**perhuman. Superpopulated.	Overpopulated	
Couche (f) d'ozone	koush-doh-zone	Une couche – a layer. You lie on a couch. A human layer on a couch.	Ozone layer	
Planète (f)	plah-net		Planet	
Ours polaire (m)	oarse poh-lair	**Urs**us Major is Latin for Big Bear, a constellation, it's not an (h)ourse, it's a bear	Polar bear	
Pollution (f)	pawl-oo-see-yaw		Pollution	
Sauvegarder (v)	sohv-gaar-day	Sauver – save, saviour. Garder – guard, look after.	Protect (v)	
Espèces rares (fpl)	ess-pess raahr	Remove the 'E' and it's virtually **spec**i**es**	Rare species	
Recyclage (m)	reuh-see-klah-zheuh	Take off the -er and add -age to the verb, recycler. You get recyclage.	Recycling	
Ressources (fpl) renouvelables	reuh-souhrs reuh-nouh-veuh-la-bleuh	Renouvelable looks like renewable. Resources of energy.	Renewable energy	
Montée des eaux (f)	mawn-tay days oh	Eau – aqua, water. Monter – to go up (a **mount**ain), to rise.	Rising water	
Ciel (m)	see-yell	**Cel**estial means 'to do with the sky', **cle**ar, **cli**mate, **cl**oudless, **ceil**ing	Sky	
Énergie (f) solaire	ay-nair-zhee soll-air	Solar power in English	Solar power	
Espace (f)	ess-pass	Lots of Renaults float around in it	Space	
Espèces (fpl)	ess-pess	E**spèce** is almost species	Species	
Étoile (f)	ay-twaahl	é denotes 's', stoile, **st**ellar, con**st**ellation	Star	
Raz-de-marée (m)	rah-deuh-mah-ray	**Mar**ée, like la **mer**, the sea, **mer**maid. Marée – tide. Raz – the **R**im. The top or the rim of the tide, is the tidal wave.	Tidal wave	

Word or phrase	Pronunciation guide	Aide-mémoire	English meaning	Check
Énergie (f) marée-motrice	ay-nair-zhee mah-ray-moh-treece	Motor power coming from the marée, the tide. **Mar**ée, like the **mer**, the sea, tide.	Tidal energy	
Sous-produits toxiques mpl	souh-prod-wee tox-eek	Sous, sub, under, under the main product, or beside, by the main product	Toxic by-products	
Sans plomb (m)	saw-plaw	Médecins **Sans** Frontières (doctors **without** borders) plumbers and lead pipes.	Unleaded	
Guerre (f)	gair	A guerrilla is a fighter in a conflict	War	
Détritus (m)	day-tree-toos	Detritus is an English word meaning waste. Looks a bit like **de**bris.	Waste (for the bin)	
Gaspillage de ressources	gas-pee-ah-zheuh deuh reuh-souhrss	**Pillage** means to wreck for the sake of wrecking. Such activity produces waste **gas**.	Waste of resources	
Vague (f)	vahg	Wave and **va**g**ue** have 3 letters in common, ave. A vague gesture can be a wave.	Wave	
Énergie (f) éolienne	ay-nair-zhee ay-oh-lee-en	'A' (h)ole, pronounced in an English cockney way (no 'h') can be related to wind.	Wind power	
Monde (m)	mawnd	The **mo**u**nd** of earth we live in is the World	World	
Mondial (aux) (e/s)	mawnd-ee-al	'Of this mound' is 'mondial', just like 'of the norm' is 'normal' and 'of the habit' is 'habitual'	Worldwide	

Practise!

1. Translate this passage including the title.

Dans un monde qui change, on doit changer!

J'habite dans un monde qui change. Je pense que ça fait un peu peur (*ça fait peur – it is scary*). Dans mon monde, nous avons beaucoup de problèmes. Par exemple, il y a beaucoup de guerres.

Il y a toujours eu des guerres (*Il y a toujours eu – there have always been*) mais maintenant, plus de personnes meurent (*meurent comes from the verb, mourir, to die*).

Aussi, l'équilibre de la planète change. Dans le passé, il faisait moins chaud. Maintenant, il y a les sécheresses et les calottes fondent. Dans le passé, il y avait assez à manger pour les ours polaires, maintenant les ours polaires meurent. On doit arrêter de faire de la pollution avec les combustibles fossiles et on doit faire de l'énergie en utilisant les ressources renouvelables.

_____

_____

_____

_____

_____

_____

_____

_____

_____

_____

12: Les espèces menacées
[Endangered species]

Word or phrase	Pronunciation guide	Aide-mémoire	English meaning	Check
Ours (m)	ouhrss	**Urs**us Major is the Latin for the Great Bear constellation. A bear is a little like a (h)orse.	Bear	
Oiseau (m)	wah-zoh	**O**c**ea**n – flying over it, flying over the **eau**, water	Bird	
Crapaud (m) à tête de boeuf	krah-poh ah tet deuh beuhff	**T**oad looks like crap**aud**. Toad crap not pretty, like the bull head (tête). Boeuf, beef, bull.	Bull head toad	
Ange (m) de mer commun	awe-zheuh deuh mair kaw-mah	**Ange**l. Mer is where the maid of the sea lives.	Common sea angel	
Dauphin (m)	doh-fah	**Dol**p**hin**	Dolphin	
Éléphant (m)	ay-lay-faw		Elephant	
Renard (f)	ren-aarh	**Ren**oune**d** for their deviousness	Fox	
Gorille (m) géant	go-ree-yeuh		Giant gorilla	
Grand requin (m) blanc	graw reuh-kah blaw	Grand – great. Mr Requin is 'wreckin' the fish stocks. Blank, white.	Great white shark	
Papillon (m) monarque	pah-pee-yaw moh-naark	'Pah pee yaw' is like the 'bah tee ying' of wings of a butterfly. Also, 2 'l's in French, 2 't's in English.	Monarch butterfly	
Singe, (m)	sah-zheuh	**Singe**d his hair **swing**ing too close to the sun	Monkey	
Panda (m)	pawn-dah		Panda	
Pingouin (m)	pah-gwah		Penguin	
Ours (m) polaire	ouhrss poh-lair	**Urs**us Major is the Latin for the Great Bear constellation. Polaire helps us understand.	Polar bear	
Rhinocéros (m)	ree-noh-say-ross		Rhinoceros	
Hippocampe (m)	ee-poh-kawmp	Hippopotamus is Greek for 'river' (potamus), 'horse' (hippo). The seahorse camps in a cave on the ocean bed.	Seahorse	
Tigre (m)	tee-greuh		Tiger	
Tortue (f)	tor-too		Tortoise	
Baleine (f)	bah-len	We have similar letters in b**ale**ine. Whalers use balers for balin' when whalin'!	Whale	
Cacatoès (m) à huppe jaune	kah-kah-toh-ess ah oop zhoan	Cacatoès is similar to cockatoo. The huppe (the crest) is 'oop' on top of his head.	Yellow-crested Cockatoo	
Chasse (f) pour nourriture	Shass pouhr nouh-ree-toohr	Chasing an animal for **nouri**shment	Hunting for food	1
Exportation (f) illégale	Eks-pohr-tass-yaw ee-lay-gahl	Export is pretty close to exportation	Illegal export	2
Habitat (m) perdu	Ah-bee-tah pair-doo	I bought a wig. I lost it. I **lost** my **hair-do**, it was **pair-du**. Without my **hair-do** I am **perdu**.	Loss of habitat	3

Practise!

Choose six animals that you think may be in danger of extinction and guess the reason why, choosing from the reasons that are noted (1, 2, 3) on the previous page.

1. Nom d'animal (français)   (English)

Raison principale (français)   (English)

2. Nom d'animal (français)   (English)

Raison principale (français)   (English)

3. Nom d'animal (français)   (English)

Raison principale (français)   (English)

4. Nom d'animal (français)   (English)

Raison principale (français)   (English)

5. Nom d'animal (français)   (English)

Raison principale (français)   (English)

6. Nom d'animal (français)   (English)

Raison principale (français)   (English)

13: Les problèmes sociaux
[Social problems]

Word or phrase	Pronunciation guide	Aide-mémoire	English meaning	Check
Toxicomane (m/f)	toxee-coh-man	Drugs are **toxic** and can put you in a **coma**	Addict	
Accro (adj)	ah-kroh	Accro is short for accroché. A **croche**t in music, like a hook. Addicted, hooked.	Addicted	
Dépendance (f) de	day-pawn-dawss deuh	If you depend on something you are addicted	Addiction to	
Alcool (m)	al-kohl		Alcohol	
Anorexie (f)	ah-noh-rek-see		Anorexia	
Boulimie (f)	bouh-lee-mee		Bulimia	
Intimidation (f)	ahn-tee-mee-dass-yaw	If you are intimidating someone, you are bullying them	Bullying	
Changement (m)	shaw-zheuh-maw	Notice that when change is a noun, it gains '-ment'	Change	
Organisation (f) caritative	oar-gah-nee-zass-yaw	A **car**ing (**car**itative) organisation	Charity (charitable organisation)	
Drogue (f) used in singular	drog	'La drogue, c'est un problème' means that 'drugs' are a problem.	Drugs (in French, used in singular)	
Toxicomanie (f)	toxee-coh-man-ee	Drugs are **toxic** can put you in a **coma**	Drug abuse	
Ivre	eev-reuh	**Ivre**, not good for the livre (the liver)	Drunk	
Pays (m) développé	pay-ee day-veuh-lop-ay	**Pa**triots, re**pa**triated (sent back to your country)	Developed country	
Pays (m) en voie de développement	pay-ee awe vwah deuh day-veuh-lop-maw	Via = road. 'Rome via (voie) Paris'. Road to development.	Developing country	
Collecte (f)	koll-ekt	La collecte means the funds that are **collecte**d	Funds collected	
Se soûler (v)	seuh souh-lay	Said drunkenly, 'i'm verrrry **souhlay** for ma behaviour'	Get drunk	
Santé (f)	sawn-tay	Sane, sanitary, healthy	Healthy	
Sans-abris (mpl)	saw-zab-ree	**Sans**-doute (without doubt). Shelters need **a bri**ck!	Homeless	
SDF (m/f) Sans Domicile Fixe	ess day eff saw dom-ee-seel feaks	Without **fixe**d abode. **Dom**icile, **dom**estic, home.	Homeless person	
Foyer (m)	fwah-yay	Foyer, the 'welcome' area of a building. Hostels welcome.	Hostel	
Aide (f) humanitaire	ed oo-man-ee-tair		Humanitarian aid	
Se faire mal	seuh fair mal	To one**self**, to do, faire (how you doin/farin?). Mal – bad.	Hurt oneself	

Word or phrase	Pronunciation guide	Aide-mémoire	English meaning	Check
Amélioration (f)	ah-may-lee-oar-ass-yaw	Ameliorate means improve. Link to **meill**eu**r** – better.	Improvement	
Blessure (f)	bless-oohr	You need **blesse**d to cure your injury	Injury	
ONG Organisation (f) non-gouvernementale	oh en zhay	Adjectives are often second in French – this is a good example	NGO	
Obésité (f)	oh-bay-see-tay		Obesity	
Cyber-intimidation (f)	see-bair ahn-tee-mee-dass-yaw	Cyber is online. Intimidation is bullying, making timid.	Online bullying	
Pression (f) des paires	press-yaw day pair	**P**ai**r**e **press**ion	Peer pressure	
Pauvre	poh-vreuh	**P**auv**r**e	Poor	
Pauvreté (f)	poh-vreuh-tay	**P**au**vret**é	Poverty	
Collecter (v) des fonds	kall-ek-tay day faw	**Collect**er **f**o**nds**	Raise money (funds)	
Taux (m) de chômage	toh deuh show-mah-zheuh	**Ta**lly, taux, rate. 'Chô-me the way to the job centre!'	Rate of unemployment	
Résolution (f) de conflit	ray-zoh-loose-yaw deuh kaw-flee	**Confli**ct	Resolution of conflict	
Bidonville (f)	bee-daw-veel	A 'bidon' is a tin, and 'ville' is town (**vill**age). Tintown.	Slum	
Tabagisme (m)	tah-bah-zhees-meuh	**T**a**ba**gisme looks like tobacco	Smoking	
Tiers (m) monde	tee-air mawnd	Tiers, **Tear**fund, tiers like **t**hi**r**d. **Mo**und of Earth, world.	Third World	
Malsain(s)/malsaine(s)	mahl-sah/malsen	Mal, **mal**icious, **mal**ignant. Sain, **san**e, healthy.	Unhealthy	
Chômage (m)	show-mah-zheuh	Chô-me the way to a job, or Chô Madge, she needs one too!	Unemployment	
Bénévolat (m)	bay-nay-voh-lah	'Béné', good. **Bene**fit. '**Vol**', of ones volition, you want to.	Voluntary work	
Bénévole (m)	bay-nay-vall	'Béné', good. **Bene**fit. '**Vol**', of ones volition, you want to.	Volunteer	

Practise!

The English phrases in the second column below are in the correct order to form a passage of text. However, the French phrases in the first column are in a random order. Re-write the French phrases in the proper order to correctly translate the English passage.

Ces jours-ci	These days	Ces jours-ci
et je crois que	there are	_____
il y a	many young people	_____
c'est très enrichissant	who want	_____
de nombreux jeunes	to do a gap year because	_____
parce que	they want to volunteer	_____
ça leur permet de	in a developing country	_____
qui veulent	and I think that	_____
voir la pauvreté	it is very rewarding	_____
faire une année sabattique car	because	_____
de leurs propres yeux	it allows them	_____
et de mieux comprendre	to see the poverty	_____
ils veulent faire du bénévolat	with their own eyes	_____
l'importance du travail	and to better understand	_____
des ONGs	the importance of the work	_____
dans un pays en voie de développement	of the NGOs	_____
et des bénévoles	and the volunteers	_____
et aussi de voir	and also to see	_____
améliorer la vie dans le Tiers Monde	that one can	_____
qu'on peut	improve life in the Third World	_____

14: La santé et le mode de vie – première partie
[Health and lifestyle – first part]

Word or phrase	Pronunciation guide	Aide-mémoire	English meaning	Check
Athlétisme (m) (faire de l')	fair deuh lat-lay-tees-meuh	Athletism ought to be our word!	Athletics	
Balle (f), ballon (m) de foot	baahl	Balle – this ball has the 'e' of t**e**nnis. It is a small ball.	Ball (small), football	
Boules (fpl) (jouer aux)	jouh-ay oh bouhl	Sounds like **bowls**	Bowls	
Pétanque (f) (jouer à la)	jouh-ay ah lah pay-tawnk	Onomatopeia. Pay-tawnk is the sound of one metal ball hitting another.	Bowls	
Canoë (m) (faire du)	fair doo kahn-way		Canoeing	
Tchacher avec les amis	cha-chay ah-vek lays amee	Tchacher – chat. Amis – amicable – friendly.	Chat online with friends	
Escalade (f) (faire de l')	fair deuh less-kah-lad	E**scal**ade, **scal**ing the rock is what we are doing here. '-ade' creates a noun.	Climbing (Rock)	
Collectionner des timbres	collec-see-yawn-ay day tam-breuh	Collectionner – collect. Timbres – s**T**imothy the s**T**amp collector.	Collect stamps	
Cricket (m) (jouer au)	jouh-ay oh kreek-ett		Cricket	
Vélo (m) (faire du)	fair doo vay-lo	Vélodrome is the cycle arena	Cycling	
Cyclisme (m) (faire du)	fair doo see-kleese-meuh		Cycling	
Cycliste (m/f)	see-kleest		Cyclist	
Danse (f) (faire de la)	fair deuh la dawhss		Dancing	
Piste (f) de danse	peast deuh dawhss	In English, we use off-piste to mean off the track. The dance track (floor).	Dance floor	
Fléchettes (fpl) (jouer aux)	jouh-ay oh flay-shet	-ette, a little thing. Une flè**che** – arrow, used in ar**che**ry. Flé**che**tte, little arrow.	Darts	
Dessiner (v)	dess-seen-ay	Design	Draw	
Dessin (m)	dess-ah	A **desi**g**n**	Drawing	
Manger	maw-zhay	Cattle eat from a manger	Eating	
Fana(tique) de	fah-nah (teek) deuh	Fan comes from fan-atical	Fan of	
Films (mpl) (Regarder les)	regard-ay lay feelm	With regard to something means 'looking at something'; regarding you – looking at you.	Films	
Pêche (f) (aller à la)	allay ah lah pesh	**Pi**ck a fish from the water. It's a **pe**a**ch**! **Pi**s**ce**s, zodiac. **P**os**e**idon, the sea god.	Fishing	
Football (m) (jouer au)	jouh-ay oh foot-ball		Football	
Jeu (m)	zheu	Jouer is to play. The joy of play. Jeu is the noun, a game.	Game	
Partie (f)	paar-tee	It is not winning the game that counts, it is **parti**cipating!	Game (match, clash)	
Jardinage (m) (faire du)	fair doo zhaahr-dee-nah-zheuh	Jardin looks and sounds like garden	Gardening	

Word or phrase	Pronunciation guide	Aide-mémoire	English meaning	Check
Sortir avec mes amis	sore-teer ah-vek may zamee	Sort **out** with your amiable friends. A sortie is a **out**ing made by a jet fighter.	Go out with friends	
Golf (m) (jouer au)	jouh-ay oh golf		Golf	
Guitare (f) (jouer de la)	jouh-ay deuh lah geet-aar		Guitar	
Gymnase (m)	zheem-nazz		Gymnasium (gym)	
Marcher dans les montagnes	maar-shay daw lay mawn-tah-nyeuh	Marching is walking	Hill-walking	
Passe-temps (mpl)	pass-taw	Pass-time. Tempus fugit = time flies in Latin. Temporary, to do with time.	Hobby	
Équitation (f) (faire de l')	fair deuh lay-key-tass-yaw	Equestrian, equine, to do with horses	Horse-riding	
Patinoire (f)	pah-teen-wire	-oir, a place, abattoir. A dog skates on **pa**ws. I'm **patti**ng him – if I catch him!	Ice-rink	
Patinage (m) (faire du)	fair doo pah-tee-nah-zheuh	A dog skates on **pa**ws. I like **patting** him, if I can catch him. -age for a noun.	Ice-skating	
Footing (m) (faire du)	fair doo footing	Footing – jogging	Jogging	
Écouter la musique	ay-kouh-tay lah moo-zeek	An **ec**ho is a sound that you listen for. **Musi**que to my ears.	Listen to music	
Match (m)	match		Match	
VTT (faire du)	fair doo vay tay tay	Vélo Tout Terrain. **V**elodrome – bike. **T**out – total, all. **T**errain – all-terrain biking.	Mountain biking	
Alpinisme (faire de l')	fair deuh lalp-ee-neese-meuh	The Alps. Alpinism is not an addiction to breakfast cereal. Ha!	Mountaineering	

Practise!

Decide if each word above is related to an outdoor or indoor activity, or if it is a word that can be in either category. Write the words, in French, inside the Venn diagram.

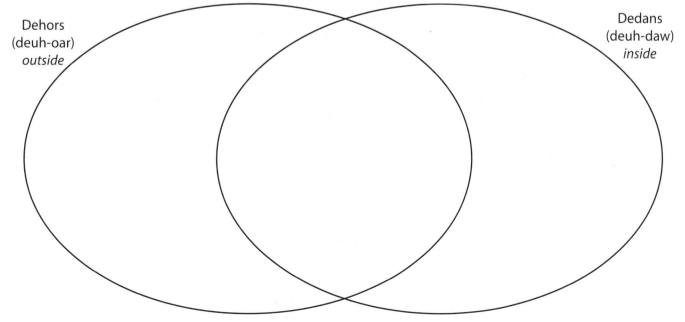

Dehors
(deuh-oar)
outside

Dedans
(deuh-daw)
inside

15: La santé et le mode de vie – deuxième partie
[Health and lifestyle – second part]

Word or phrase	Pronunciation guide	Aide-mémoire	English meaning	Check
Filet (m)	fee-lay	Filay your netay with fishay. Fil**et** link to n**et**.	Net	
Plein air (m) (être en plein air)	et-reuh awe plahn-air	Plein – full, as in re**plen**ished. Full air can only be found outside, in the open.	Open air	
Excursion (f) au ciné	excur-see-yaw oh see-nay	An excursion is an outing to the **ciné**ma	Outing to cinema	
Photographie (f) (Faire de la)	fair de la fo-to-gra-fee		Photography	
Piano (m) (jouer du)	jouh-ay doo pee-ah-noh		Piano	
Randonnées (f) (faire des)	(fair day) rawn-dawn-ay	**Ra**mbl**es** are walks	Rambling	
Lire (v)	lear	A **lectu**re is a reading, **lyri**cs are words	Read	
Lecture (f) (faire de la)	fair deuh lah lek-toor	A **lectu**re is a reading, **lyri**cs are words	Reading	
Roller (m) (faire du)	fair doo roh-leuhr	Roller without the blade	Roller-blading	
Patin (m) à roulettes (faire du)	fair doo pah-tah ah rouh-let	Swiss dog, skates on **pa**ws. I like **patti**ng him, if I catch him. Skates **roll**ing.	Roller-skating	
Rugby (m) (jouer au)	jouh-ay oh roog-bee		Rugby	
Voile (f) (faire de la)	fair deuh lah vwaahl	A big **veil** attached to a mast is a sail	Sailing	
Plongée (f) sous-marine (faire de la)	fair deuh lah plaw-zhay souh-maar-een	Plunging, **s**o**u**s = **su**b = under. Marine – to do with the mer, sea.	Scuba diving	
Vendre des choses (fpl)	vawn-dreuh day shows	Vending machine, vendor. Cosa nostra – our thing. I chose shows!	Sell things	
Séries (fpl) (regarder les)	regard-ay lay say-ree		Series	
Shopping (m) (faire du)	fair doo shop-ping		Shopping	
Chanter	shawn-tay	Chanting is singing	Sing	
Skate (m) (faire du)	fair doo skate	Remember it's **skate**boarding, not skating!	Skateboarding	
Planche (f) à roulettes	plaw-sheuh ah rouh-let	A **pla**tter is a tray, a board. Roulettes, like little rollers under your board.	Skateboard	
Sportif/sportive (adj)	spor-teef/spor-teeve		Sporty	
Stade (m)	stad	**Stad** without the ium	Stadium	
Rester à la maison	res-tay ah la may-zaw	Staying at home for a rest. Maison – mansion – house – home.	Stay at home	
Supporter (m/f)	soo-pore-tair		Supporter	
(Faire de la) natation (f)	fair deuh la nat-tass-yaw	**Na**vy, **na**utical – to do with water	Swimming	
Nager dans la piscine	nah-zhay daw lah pea-seen	**Na**vy, **na**utical – to do with water. Piscine – this can happen in one!	Swim in the pool	
Nager dans la mer	nah-zhay daw lah mare	**Na**vy, **na**utical – to do with water. Mermaid – maid of the sea.	Swim in the sea	

Word or phrase	Pronunciation guide	Aide-mémoire	English meaning	Check
Bronzer à côté de la piscine	braw-zay ah coh-tay deuh la pea-seen	Côté – the ô indicates an 's' after the o, so 'coste', like coast, like sea-side	Tan beside the pool	
Equipe (f) (faire partie d'une)	fair paahr-tee doon ay-keep	A team is comprised of human positional **equip**ment. **Ay keep** winning!	Team	
Piste (f)	peast	In English we use 'off-piste' to talk about skiing not on a designated track	Track (for skiing)	
Entraînement (m) (faire de l')	fair deuh law-tren-maw	En**train**ement. '-ment' indicates a noun. **Train**ing.	Training	
Formation (faire une)	fair oon for-mass-yaw	Formation, formal training, e.g. teacher training. To form is to shape, train.	Training	
Voyager	vwhy-aa-zhay	French expression: 'Les voyages forment la jeunesse!' Traveling shapes youth.	Travel	
Jeux (mpl) vidéo (jouer aux)	jouh-ay oh jeuh vee-day-oh	**Joue**r – to play, the **jo**y of play. Un jeu – a game.	Video games	
Volley (m) (jouer au)	jouh-ay oh vawl-ay	Volleyball without the ball	Volleyball	
Promenade (f) (faire une)	fair oon prom-en-ad	A promenade is a walkway by the sea	Walk	
Promenades (fpl) (faire des) en ville	fair day prom-en-add awe veal	A promenade is a walkway by a beach. En ville, in the village? Nope – it's down in the downtown.	Walks downtown	
Sports (mpl) aquatiques	sporze ah-kwah-teek	Aquatic, to do with water	Water sports	
Travailler dans le jardin	trav-eye-yeah daw leuh jaahr-dah	To test ability to work, you are put on trial. Travails – old word for labour/work.	Work in the garden	
Faire du lèche-vitrines (m)	fair du lesh vee-treen	**Le**c**h**er, to **lic**k, **vi**t**rin**e, **vin**dow, literally window licking, drooling with desire	Window shopping	
Planche (f) à voile (faire de la)	fair deuh lah plawsh ah vwaal	A **pla**tter is a tray, a board. Voile is a veil, a sail.	Windsurfing	

Practise!

Décidez si les mots sont sportifs, non-sportifs ou si les mots peuvent être considérés comme l'un ou l'autre (*l'un ou l'autre – one or the other*). Écrivez-les en français dans le diagramme de Venn.

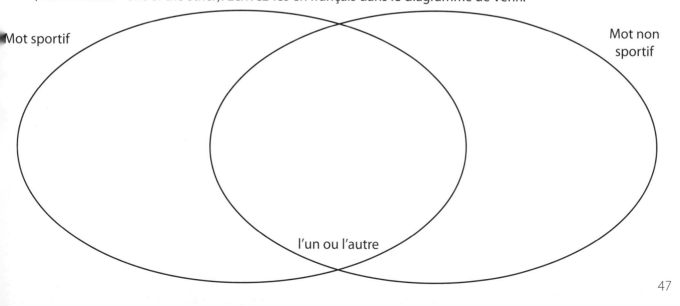

Mot sportif

Mot non sportif

l'un ou l'autre

16: La nourriture et les boissons
(Food and drink)

Quelques ingrédients de base *(Some basic ingredients)*

Word or phrase	Pronunciation guide	Aide-mémoire	English meaning	Check
Nourriture (f) de base	nouh-ree-too-reuh deuh bazz	Basic nourishment	Basic food	
Pain (m)	pah	Bread in '**pan**try'. The Breadfather, 'Panda' – Get It? Pan – bread, da – father! Com**pan**ion.	Bread	
Frites (fpl)	freet	**Frie**d, deep fried potato chips are crisps	Chips	
Farine (f)	fah-reen	**F**lo**ur**, starting letter. You won't get **far**-in bread-making without flour.	Flour	
Sauce (f)	sohsse	Sauce from cooking juices is called….	Gravy	
Moutarde (f)	mouh-taard	**M**o**utard**e	Mustard	
Nouilles (fpl)	nouh-yeuh	**No**ui**lles**	Noodles	
Huile (f) d'olive	lweel doh-leev	Oil is useful on a wheel, also 'h_**uil**_e' (looks, sounds like oil). 'Olive' aids understanding.	Olive oil	
Pâtes (fpl)	pat	The â denotes that an 's' follows	Pasta	
Poivre (m)	pwah-vreuh	**P**oiv**r**e	Pepper	
Pommes (fpl) de terre	pawm deuh tair	Pom-pom, apple-shaped, on a woolly hat, of the terrain, ground, apple of the ground	Potatos	
Riz (m)	ree	**Ri**ce	Rice	
Sel (m)	sell	**S**a**l**t	Salt	
Spaghettis (fpl)	spaag-ett-ee		Spaghetti	
Bouillon (m)	bouh-wee-yaw	**Bo**u**il**ing bones gives you this	Stock	
Sucre (f)	soo-kreuh	**Su**g**ar**	Sugar	
Huile (f) de tournesol	weel deuh touhr-neuh-sol	Oil is useful on a wheel, also h_**uil**_e. Tournesol – turn solar, sunflower.	Sunflower oil	
Ketchup (m)	ketch-up		Tomato ketchup	
Vinaigre (m)	vee-nai-greuh	Looks like (and actually means) vin aigre – wine sour, which is sour wine, which is vinegar	Vinegar	

Les produits laitiers (Dairy products)

Word or phrase	Pronunciation guide	Aide-mémoire	English meaning	Check
Beurre (m)	beuhrr	**Beur**re	Butter	
Petit lait (m)	ptee-lay	Small milk	Buttermilk	
Fromage (m)	froh-ma-zheuh	From-ages past we've been eating cheese	Cheese	
Crème (f) chantilly	crem shawn-tee-yee	Crème, sp**ill**. The sort of cream you can spilly is Chantilly.	Cream (for dessert)	
Crème (f) anglaise	crem awn-glezz	English cream is custard, a very English product	Custard	
Produits (mpl) laitiers	prod-wee lay-tee-ay	**La**it – **la**ctose, to do with milk	Dairy products	
Œuf (mpl)	ahn euhff	Starting letter vowel, short word	Egg	
Œufs (mpl)	euh	Starting letter vowel, short word	Eggs	
Margarine (f)	maar-gaar-een		Margarine	
Lait (m)	lay	Lactose	Milk	
Yaourt (m)	yah-ouhrt		Yoghurt	

Practise!

Find three edible combinations and three disgusting combinations, where you take one element in French from basic ingredients and one from dairy products in French and mix them together.

Mangeable (edible)

1. _____ et _____

2. _____ et _____

3. _____ et _____

Dégoûtant (disgusting)

1. _____ et _____

2. _____ et _____

3. _____ et _____

17: La viande et le poisson
[Meat and fish]

Word or phrase	Pronunciation guide	Aide-mémoire	English meaning	Check
Bacon (m)	bay-con		Bacon	
Boucherie (f)	booh-shair-ee	Butcher, because it feeds your 'bouche' mouth	Butchers	
Côte (f)	koat	**Ch**o**p**, same amount of letters	Chop	
Poisson (m)	pwah-saw	Pisces, poseidon	Fish	
Cuisses (f) de Grenouille	kweese deuh greuh-nouh-wee-yeuh	Geese have incweesed (in**cuisse**d) the size of their thighs. Is 'gren' the colour of that animal? Oui! – Gren oui!	Frogs' legs (thighs)	
Jambon (m)	zhawm-baw	G**amm**on is ham and is pretty close to this	Ham	
Agneau (m)	an-yoh	Agnes is the name of that little lamb. The lamb is called **Agne**s. Oh!	Lamb	
Lardons (mpl)	laarh-daw	Lard is animal fat, at least that is linked	Little bits of bacon	
Homard (m)	oh-maahr	Pay **hom**age to the lobster **ar** else!	Lobster	
Viande (f)	vee-awnd	'Victuals' is an old word for meat. **Vi**tal for living. La **vi**e – life.	Meat	
Viande (f) hachée	vee-yawned ahs-ay	A **ha**t**che**t can be used to cut up meat thinly, like this product	Mince	
Côtelettes (fpl) de porc	coat-let-deuh pore	'Porc' helps. Côte – side, edge (like coast). Side of pork, pork cutlet.	Pork cutlet	
Crêvette (f)	crev-et	**Cr**awfish, **cr**ab, **cr**ustacean, crevette! A Prince song: Little red crevette!	Prawn	
Saucisson (m)	soh-see-saw	Looks like **saus**age	Salami, cold sausage	
Saumon (m)	soh-maw	**Sa**u**mon**	Salmon	
Saucisse (f)	soh-seese		Sausage	
Escargot (m)	ess-car-goh	Look how slow does the S Car Go!	Snail	
Produits (mpl) à base de soja	prod-wee ah bazz deuh soh-zhah		Soya based products	
Steak (m)	stake		Steak	
Thon (m)	taw	Tuna don't wear **thon**gs	Tuna	
Dinde, (f)	daand	Dandering around like a turkey. **Din**nde**r**.	Turkey	
Escalope (f) de veau	ess-kah-lohp deuh voh	A cut of meat is esca**lop**ped off the **vea**l (**vea**u). Veal is a cow calf.	Veal chop	
Végétalien(ne) (m/f)	vay-zhay-tah-lee-ah, vay-zhay-tah-lee-enn	Italian vegetarian, a vegan	Vegan	
Végétarien(ne) (m/f)	vay-zhay-tah-ree-ah, vay-zhay-tah-ree-enn		Vegetarian	
Végétarisme (m)	vay-zhay-tah-reeze-meuh	Careful (in French, 'Ian' is not a vegetarian! Végétar isme).	Vegetarianism	

Practise!

Go through the list of words and make a list, in French and English, of the living creatures. There are nine. List them in order from what you think would be smallest, to the biggest.

Français   Anglais

1. _____   _____

2. _____   _____

3. _____   _____

4. _____   _____

5. _____   _____

6. _____   _____

7. _____   _____

8. _____   _____

9. _____   _____

18: Chez l'épicier
[At the grocer's]

Word or phrase	Pronunciation guide	Aide-mémoire	English meaning	Check
Betterave (f)	bet-rahv	Starting letter, **beet**root. "Better 'ave" a beetroot.	Beetroot	
Biscuit (m)	beese-kwee		Biscuit	
Broccolis (mpl)	broh-koh-lee		Broccoli	
Chou (m) de Bruxelles	shouh deuh brooks-el	Chou – a cabbage, therefore this is a Brussels cabbage. A sprout is a small cabbage.	Brussels sprout	
Céréales (fpl)	say-ray-al		Cereals	
Cacao (m)	kah-kah-oh		Cocoa	
Chou (m)	shouh	Link to Brussels cabbage, minus Brussels. Petit chou – little darling!	Cabbage	
Carotte (f)	kah-rot		Carrot	
Chou-fleur (m)	shouh-fleuhr	Chou – cabbage. Fleur – flower. Cabbage-flower.	Cauliflower	
Céleri (m)	sale-ree		Celery	
Concombre (m)	kaw-kawm-breuh		Cucumber	
Ail, de l'ail (m)	eye, deuh-lye	Good for preventing ailments, especially vampire-related **ail**ments	Garlic	
Haricots (mpl) verts	ah-ree-koh vair	Vert, verdant, green. A bean pod is like a cot, a **hairy cot** for green beans.	Green beans	
Provisions, (fpl)	proh-veese-yaw	Provisions are groceries, foodstuff.	Groceries, foodstuff	
Épicier (m)	ay-pee-see-yay	They originally sold spices. 'é' at the start of a word replaces 's'. Spice shop, grocers'.	Grocery shop	
Alimentation (f)	aal-ee-mawn-tass-yaw	Food (groceries) are the base a**liments** (elements) of life	Grocery shop, food	
Fines herbes (fpl)	feen-zairb	Fine herbs	Herbs	
Miel (m)	mee-yell	It is a **me**al for bees and they make a miel of it!	Honey	
Confiture (f)	kaw-fee-toohr	Jam is a **conf**ec**ti**onary product	Jam	
Laitue (f)	lay-tooh	**Lai**tue, looks like	Lettuce	
Champignon (m)	shawm-peen-yaw	Not 'mush room' for a champion in here!	Mushroom	
Oignon (m)	on-yaw		Onion	
Petits pois (mpl)	peuh-tee pwah	A lot of '**p's**, they aren't big	Peas	
Poivrons (mpl)	pwaahv-raw	**P**oiv**r**o**ns**, some similarity of spelling. Linked to poivre – pepper (condiment), like English.	Peppers	
Pomme de terre (f)	pawm deuh tair	Pom-pom, apple-like, of the territory, ground, apple of the ground	Potato	
Citrouille (f)	see-trouh-ee-yeuh	**Ci**nderel**l**a used one as a carriage	Pumpkin	

Word or phrase	Pronunciation guide	Aide-mémoire	English meaning	Check
Crudités (fpl)	kroo-dee-tay	Crude is unrefined, natural, uncooked. Crude oil, unrefined, untreated, raw.	Raw vegetables	
Salade (f)	salaad		Salad	
Épice (f)	ay-peese	'é' at the start of a word replaces 's'	Spice	
Épicé(e/s)	ay-pee-say	'é' at the start of a word replaces 's'. 'é' at the end often replaces 'y', e.g. risqué, épicé.	Spicy	
Épinards (mpl)	ay-pee-naahr	'é' at the start of a word replaces 's'. **Spina**rds.	Spinach	
Maïs (m)	my-eese	Maize	Sweetcorn	
Boîte (f)	bwaaht	Letters are a mixture of **bo**x and **ti**n. Store things in the **bo**ot of the car. Box at back.	Tin/can/box	
Légumes (mpl)	lay-goom	When in a plane, long vegetables need a lot of 'leg-oom'.	Vegetables	

Practise!

Make up two stir fry recipes using the items in this section. Each recipe should include five or more items. One recipe should be delicious, the other horrible! The names of the items themselves should be written in French but you can provide the instructions in English (in French if you feel able!)

For example, for the delicious one:

Fry some 'onions', some 'champignons' and some 'ail'. Then add some 'fines herbes'.

Serve on top of some 'laitue'.

1. Delicious

_____

_____

_____

2. Horrible

_____

_____

_____

19: Les fruits
[Fruits]

Word or phrase	Pronunciation guide	Aide-mémoire	English meaning	Check
Pomme (f)	pawm	A pom-pom is an apple-shaped addition to a woolly hat	Apple	
Abricot (m)	ab-ree-coh		Apricot	
Banane (f)	bah-naan		Banana	
Mûre (f)	moohr	Mûre berries needed, so go and pick 'em!	Blackberry	
Cassis (m)	kah-seese	Crème de cassis is a blackcurrant liqueur. Who nicked Cassi's blackcurrant?	Blackcurrant	
Myrtille (f)	day meer-tee-yeuh	Myrtle the blueberry picker!	Blueberry	
Cerise (f)	seuh-reeze	Looks like	Cherry	
Noix (f) de coco	nwah deuh koh-koh		Coconut	
Fruits (mpl)	fruh-wee		Fruits	
Pamplemousse (m)	pawm-pleuh-mousse	'Pample', a huge pimple-mouse, ate my grapefruit!	Grapefruit	
Raisins (mpl)	day ray-zah	Dried grapes are raisins	Grapes	
Nectarine (f)	nek-tah-reen		Nectarine	
Orange (f)	oh-raw-zheuh		Orange	
Fruit (m) de la passion	fruh-wee deuh lah pass-yaw		Passion fruit	
Pêche (f)	pesh	Looks like	Peach	
Poire (f)	pwire	Sounds like	Pear	
Ananas (m)	ah-nah-nass	**Anna** h**as pine**d for her **apple**	Pineapple	
Prune (f)	proon	A dried plum is a prune	Plum	
Pruneau (m)	proo-noh	Looks like it	Prune	
Framboise (f)	frawm-bwazz	Similar to the **fra**ish cream ones, **bois** (boys)! (See entry below, for fraises.)	Raspberry	
Fraise (f)	frezz	Nice with **frais**h cream, brother! **Fria**r (Brother) Tuck eats Strawberries.	Strawberry	
Tomate (f)	toh-mat		Tomato	
Pastèque (f)	pass-tek	**Pass te k...**etchup to put on my watermelon!	Watermelon	

Practise!

Make a few smoothies:

1. Nom _____ Ingrédients: _____ , _____ ,

_____ , _____ , _____

2. Nom _____ Ingrédients: _____ , _____ ,

_____ , _____ , _____

3. Nom _____ Ingrédients: _____ , _____ ,

_____ , _____ , _____

20: Les boissons
[Drinks]

Word or phrase	Pronunciation guide	Aide-mémoire	English meaning	Check
Boisson (f) alcoolisée	bwah-saw al-kawl-ee-zay	**Alcoholi**c beverage	Alcoholic drink	
Bière (f)	bee-yair	Looks like	Beer	
Bouteille (f) de coca	bouh-tay-yeuh deuh koh-kah	**Bo**ut**eille**	Bottle of Coca-Cola	
Cidre (m)	see-dreuh	Looks like	Cider	
Café (m)	kaah-fay	Pretty similar	Coffee	
Boisson (f)	bwah-saw	**B**everage starts with 'b' and means 'drink'	Drink	
Boisson (f) gazeuse	bwah-saw gah-zeuhze	**Ga**ssy **b**everage	Fizzy drink	
Jus (m) de pamplemousse	zhoo deuh pawm-pleuh-mousse	'Pample', a huge pimple-mouse, ate my grapefruit	Grapefruit juice	
Chocolat (m) chaud	shock-oh-lah shoh	Chaud – a chauffeur – someone who heats a car seat for a passenger	Hot chocolate	
Limonade (f)	lee-mawn-add	Seriously similar	Lemonade	
Thé (m) au citron	tay oh seet-raw	Citric acid, lemon juice	Lemon tea	
Eau (f) minérale	oh mee-nay-raal	Eau – three vowels which run together like running water	Mineral water	
Sirop (m) à la menthe	see-roh ah lah mawnt	Syrup (sirop) is like cordial. Menthe – menthol – mint.	Mint cordial	
Jus (m) d'orange	zhoo door-aw-zheuh		Orange juice	
Jus (m) d'ananas	zhoo dah-nah-nass	Ananas – means 'excellent fruit' in Tupi, the indigenous language of Brazil. If you sat on one, it would be sore, on-an-ass! A pain-apple!	Pineapple juice	
Citron (m) pressé	seet-raw press-ay	Pressed means squeezed. They used to press grapes with their feet, to get the juice out.	Squeezed lemon juice	
Diabolo (m) fraise	dee-ah-boh-loh frezz	Diabolo – the sparkly little devil in the drink (diabolical). **Fra**i**se** – four letters are the same.	Strawberry lemonade	
Alcool (m) fort	ahl-kawl fore	Fort – strong like a fortress	Strong alcohol	
Thé (m)	tay	Pretty similar	Tea	
Vin (m)	vah	Looks like and is used in vinaigre – vinegar – 'sour wine'	Wine	

Practise!

Here is a group of people. Choose which drink they are each going to have. Write the name of the drink beside each person, in French and in English:

1. Un arrière grand-père, âgé de 93 ans, après son dîner. (A great-grandfather, 93 years old, after his dinner):

    Français _____ Anglais _____

2. Une petite fille, âgée de 6 ans, après son dîner. (A little girl, aged 6, after her dinner):

    Français _____ Anglais _____

3. Une petite fille, qui a six ans, pendant son dîner. (A little girl, who is 6, during her dinner):

    Français _____ Anglais _____

4. Un jeune jamaïquain, âgé de 22 ans, qui a soif. (A young Jamaican man, 22, who is thirsty):

    Français _____ Anglais _____

5. Un Inuit, âgé de 35 ans. (An Inuit, aged 35):

    Français _____ Anglais _____

6. Une jeune dame, âgée de 24 ans, qui est sortie faire la fête. (A young lady, aged 24, who has gone out to party):

    Français _____ Anglais _____

7. Une grand-mère qui a 75 ans, avant de se coucher. (A grand-mother, who is 75, before she goes to bed):

    Français _____ Anglais _____

8. Un garçon de 14 ans avec son Big Mac. (A 14 year old boy, with his Big Mac):

    Français _____ Anglais _____

9. Ton oncle Bill, quand il se lève le matin. (Your uncle Bill, when he gets up in the morning):

    Français _____ Anglais _____

21. Les repas et les plats
(Meals and dishes)

Word or phrase	Pronunciation guide	Aide-mémoire	English meaning	Check
Goûter (m)	gouh-tay	û denotes an 's', hence 'gusting'. **Dis**gusting means contrary to one's taste. Gusting = a tasty snack.	Afternoon snack	
Boeuf (m) Bourgignon	beuhff bore-geen-yaw	Beef – looks like	Bourgignon-style beef	
Petit-déjeuner (m)	peuh-tee day-zheuh-nay	Small breaking of fast. Jeûner – to fast, the 'dé' reverses the verb, break-fast.	Breakfast	
Tarte (f) Tatin	tart tah-tah	The Tatin sisters invented this by accident. I know that doesn't help.	Caramelised apple pie	
Coq (m) au vin	kaw-koh-vah	Cockerel is a chicken and vin is wine	Chicken in red wine	
Mousse (f) au chocolat	mousse oh shock-oh-lah		Chocolate mousse	
Crème (f) brûlée	krem broo-lay	**Bur**ned cream is what it is	Crème brûlée	
Croque-madame (m)	croc-madam	Croque-monsieur with an egg – eggs linked to woman, Madam	Croque-monsieur with egg	
Dîner (m)	dee-nay		Dinner	
Plat (m)	plah	Plate	Dish (a type of meal)	
Escalope (f) de veau	ess-kah-lope deuh voh	**Vea**u looks like veal. An esca**lop**e is **lop**ped off the animal.	Fillet of veal	
Croque-monsieur (m)	croc-meuhss-yeuhr	Croquette – a thing you eat. Croquer – to crunch, a gentleman's lunch.	Ham & cheese toastie	
Soufflé (m) au citron	souh-flay oh see-traw	Ctiric acid – acid from lemons. Souff – puff, an airy dessert.	Lemon soufflé	
Petit salé (m)	peuh-tee sah-lay	Means little salted one – gammon is salty – **sal**é	Lentils and gammon	
Déjeuner (m)	day-zheuh-nay	Break – 'dé'. Jeûner – to fast.	Lunch	
Repas (m) de midi	reuh-pah deuh mee-dee	Midi: 'di' as in lundi, mardi; 'mi' – middle middle day – midday, midday meal	Lunch (midday meal)	
Repas (m)	reuh-pah	He reaps benefits from eating meals	Meal	
Île (f) flottante	eel flaw-tawnt	Î denotes i**s**le. Floating looks like flottante. Meringue island floating in custard.	Meringue in custard	
Grignoter	gree-nyawt-ay	You **gri**gn and take **note** when you nibble	Nibble	
Omelette (f)	awm-lett		Omelette	
Soupe (f) à l'oignon	souhp ah lawn-yaw		Onion soup	
Oeuf (m) poché	euhff poché	Un oeuf is an oeuf, an egg is an egg. Poché, **po**a**che**d.	Poached egg	

Word or phrase	Pronunciation guide	Aide-mémoire	English meaning	Check
Steack (m) tartare	stake taar-taar	Steack = steak = mince. The **ra**w element is in the **ar ra** of t**ar**t**ar**e.	Raw mince with egg	
Plats (mpl) cuisinés	plah kwee-zee-nay	Cuisinés, cooked (kitchen-ed). Plat – plate, dish. Ready-kitchened dishes.	Ready-made meals	
Poulet (m) rôti	pouh-lay roh-tee	Poultry. The ô denotes an 's' after the 'o', rosti – roasty.	Roast chicken	
Rôti (m) de beouf	roh-tee deuh beuhff	ô denotes an 's' after the 'o', rosti. **Bo**e**uf** – beef.	Roast, joint of beef	
Casse-croûte (m)	kass-krouht	**Cass**trophes break things. Croûte – the û denotes 's' after the 'u', crust (crouste).	Snack	
Potage (m)	poh-ta-zheuh	Made in a **pot** which might have contained cabb**age**	Soup	
Ragoût (m)	rah-gouh	Û denotes 's' after the 'u' (link to dis**gust**ing, against my taste), Ra – link to re-, re-taste. Stews tend to be tasted again, lasting several days.	Stew	
Pot (m) au feu	paw-toh-feuh	Pot on the **fire**, is what this means and it's how to cook a stew	Stew	
Souper (m)	souh-pay	**So**u**per**	Supper	

Practise!

Answer the following questions, in French, by choosing meals from the list above.

1. Qu'est-ce que tu aimerais prendre comme petit déjeuner?

_____

2. Qu'est-ce que tu aimerais choisir comme déjeuner?

_____

3. Qu'est-ce que tu aimerais avoir comme dîner?

_____

22. La boulangerie/la pâtisserie
[Bakery/Cake shop]

Word or phrase	Pronunciation guide	Aide-mémoire	English meaning	Check
Tarte (f) aux pommes	taart oh pawm	Tart. A pom-pom is a round apple-like object attached to a woolly hat.	Apple tart	
Baguette (f)	bag-ett	This word has come into English	Baguette (French stick)	
Boulangerie (f)	bouh-lawn-zhair-ee	A boulle (ball) of dough is used to make bread. '-erie' denotes a shop, like -ery.	Bakery	
Un pain (m)	pah	Bread in **pan**try, the Breadfather, **Pan**da, un pain, a big round (like Panda) loaf	Big roundish loaf	
Petit gâteau (f)	peuh-tee gah-toh	Literally means 'little cake' but the French use it to mean biscuit	Biscuit	
Gâteau (m) forêt noire	gah-toh foh-ray nwire	â denotes 's' – gastro, goes to your stomach. ê denotes 's', forest. Noir – black.	Black forest gateau	
Pain (m)	pah	Keep bread in the '**pan**try'. The Breadfather, 'Panda'.	Bread (general word)	
Brioche (f)	bree-osh	Marie-Antoinette actually said; 'Qu'ils mangent de la brioche!' (Let them eat brioches **not** 'Let them eat cake!') before throwing some over the gates to the mob.	Brioche (bun)	
Pâtisserie (f)	pah-teese-air-ee	â denotes an 's' after the 'a', therefore, pastry. '-erie', denoting a shop.	Cake shop	
Tarte (f) aux cerises	taart aux cerises	Cerise, looks and sounds like cherries.	Cherry tart	
Éclair (m) au chocolat	ay-clair oh shock-oh-lah	Éclair has come into English. Éclair – lightning, the streak of chocolate icing on the top.	Chocolate éclair	
Éclair (m) au café	ay-clair oh kah-fay	Éclair has come into English. Éclair – lightning, the streak of coffee icing on the top.	Coffee éclair	
Croissants (mpl)	krwaah-saw		Croissants	
Galette (f) des rois	gah-lett day rwah	-ette denotes 'little' e.g. fillette, little girl. Little ga – cake, made for **ro**yal (king).	Kings' cake (frangipane)	
Mousse (f) au citron	mousse oh seet-raw	Citric acid found in lemons. Mousse is a French word in English.	Lemon mousse	
Pain (m) au chocolat	pah oh shock-oh-lah		Pain au chocolat	
Tarte (f) aux fraises	taart oh frezz	It's a tart of some description. Fraise, they are nice with fraish cream, brother.	Strawberry tart	
Pain (m) aux raisins	pah oh ray-zah	Bread in **pan**try, the Breadfather, **Pan**da. Raisins are grapes or raisins in French.	Sweet raisin bread	
Ficelle (f)	fee-sell	A **fil**ament (**fice**lle) is a thin line. A thin, fine line loaf (narrower than baguette).	Thin baguette	

Practise!

Souvent, en France, les boulangeries et les pâtisseries sont dans le même magasin. (*Often, in France, bakeries and cake shops are in the same shop*). Toutefois, vous devez faire deux listes. (*However, you must make two lists*). Une liste de produits de boulangerie et une autre liste de produits de pâtisserie. Mettez un prix pour chaque produit. (*Put a price for each product.*)

1. Boulangerie (produit en français et en anglais)   Prix

_____   _____   _____

_____   _____   _____

_____   _____   _____

_____   _____   _____

_____   _____   _____

_____   _____   _____

_____   _____   _____

2. Pâtisserie (produit en français et en anglais)   Prix

_____   _____   _____

_____   _____   _____

_____   _____   _____

_____   _____   _____

_____   _____   _____

_____   _____   _____

_____   _____   _____

23: Des bonbons, des chips et de la glace
[Sweets, crisps and ice-cream]

Word or phrase	Pronunciation guide	Aide-mémoire	English meaning	Check
Chips (fpl) saveur bacon	sheeps sah-veuhr bay-cawn	Saveur – to savour, enjoy the taste, flavour	Bacon flavour crisps	
Glace (f) à la banane	glass ah lah bah-naan		Banana flavour ice cream	
Glace (f) aux myrtilles	oh meer-tee-yeuh	Myrtille is a blueberry picker, do you know Myrtille? She picks blueberries.	Blueberry flavour	
Bonbons (mpl) durs	baw-baw doohr	Bonbons are sweets, durable, hard, boiled sweets	Boiled sweets	
Carambar (m)	cah-rawm-baahr	**Cara**mel **bar**	Chewy candy	
Chocolat (m)	shock-oh-lah		Chocolate	
Tablette (f) de chocolat	tah-blet deuh shock-oh-lah	A tablet is a square or rectangular bar	Chocolate bar	
Glace (f) au chocolat	oh shock-oh-lah		Chocolate flavour ice cream	
Chips (f)	sheeps	Careful, this is a false friend. Chips are not chips, they are crisps.	Crisps	
Chips (fpl) nature	sheeps nah-toohr	Nature – natural, without flavouring	Crisps, ready-salted	
Petit délice (m)	peuh-tee day-leese	Delicious	Delicacy	
Chewing gum (m)	shew-wing gum		Gum	
Glace (f) au rayon de miel	oh ray yaw deuh mee-yell	Bees make a **miel** of honey under the **rayon**s of the sun	Honeycomb flavour ice cream	
Glace (f) à l'eau	glass ah loh	Eau, aqua, water	Ice lolly	
Glace (f) au citron	oh see-traw	Citric acid comes from a lemon	Lemon flavour ice cream	
Petits fours (mpl)	peuh-tee fouhr	**Four** rings above an **oven**. Little things in the oven, little snacks.	Little snacks	
Amuse-gueules (mpl)	ah-mooze geuhl	**G**ow**l** is a dog's mouth, something to amuse the mouth, a little snack	Little snacks	
Sucette (f)	sooh-set	You **suc**k a lollipop	Lollipop	
Malabar (m)	mah-lah–baahr	**M**a**l** – milk. **Bar** – chew, sweet.	Malabar, milk chew	
Glace (f) à la menthe	ah lah mawnt	**M**e**nt**he, **menth**ol is mint flavour	Mint flavour ice cream	
Bonbons (mpl) à la menthe	baw-baw ah-lah-mawnt	Strawberry bonbons, blue bonbons	Mint sweet	
Sorbet (m) à l'orange	soar-bay ah low-raw-zheuh		Orange sorbet	

Word or phrase	Pronunciation guide	Aide-mémoire	English meaning	Check
Cacahuètes (fpl)	caca-wet	Ar**ach**ides are peanuts. 'Caca' suggests, among other things, 'crunch'.	Peanuts	
Glace (f) à la framboise	ah lah frawm-bwazz	Like strawberries, **fra**mbo**ise**, but the 'b' is the upside down 'p' from ras**p**berry.	Raspberry flavour ice cream	
Chips (fpl) saveur sel et vinaigre	sheeps sah-veuhr sell ay vee-neah-greuh	Sel – **sal**t, **salé** (salted). Chips are not chips, they are crisps.	Salt and vinegar flavour crisps	
Glace (f) à la fraise	ah lah frezz	St**ra**wberry ice cream is **frais**ing cold	Strawberry flavour ice cream	
Glace (f) à la vanille	glass ah lah vah nee-yeuh		Vanilla ice cream	
Noix (fpl)	nwaah	**No**ix helps. Same number of letters and the vowel sounds similar.	(Wal)nuts	

Practise!

Translate the following interesting combinations into English.

1. Une glace à la vanille et au bacon s'il vous plaît.

_____

2. Une glace qu'on peut mâcher comme le chewing gum.

_____

3. Une glace au chocolat et au vinaigre.

_____

4. Les bonbons durs saveur sel.

_____

5. Un sorbet au sel et aux myrtilles.

_____

6. Une sucette au bacon.

_____

24: Au restaurant
[At the restaurant]

Word or phrase	Pronunciation guide	Aide-mémoire	English meaning	Check
Panier (m)	pah-nee-ay	Pan is related to bread, (pain au chocolat). -ier, a recepticle. The word panier, basket, literally means bread-holder.	Basket	
Addition (f)	ah-deese-yaw	The **addi**ng up at the end of a meal	Bill	
Petit déjeuner (m)	peuh-tee day-zheunay	Jeûner – to fast. Dé- reverses the meaning. Break-fast. Petit, small(er meal).	Breakfast	
Casserole (f)	kass-air-oll	Means casserole (food) or saucepan	Casserole, stew, saucepan	
À la carte (f)	ah lah kaahrt	On the **car**d, the card that you are given to show food choices in a restaurant	Choice from the menu	
Crêpe (f)	krep	Well-known french pancake, yummy thing. ê denotes 's' after, **cris**py (thin).	Crêpe (pancake)	
Curry (m)	kooh-ree		Curry	
Dessert (m)	dess-air		Dessert	
Plat (m) du jour	plah-doo-zhouhr	**Plat**e of the jour (day) as in bon-jour, good-day.	Dish of the day	
Dégoûtant (e/s)	day-gouh-taw	û denotes an 's' after, therefore **dé**goûstant. Also, -ant often denotes -ing.	Disgusting	
Nourriture (f)	nouh-ree-toohr	**Nouri**shment is food	Food	
Frais (fraîche)	fray (fresh)	The feminine version, fraîche, sounds just like fresh	Fresh	
Faim (f)	fah	**Fam**ine, **fam**ished. In French, 'I have hunger', 'j'ai faim', means 'I'm hungry'.	Hunger (hungry)	
Plat (m) principal	plah prah-see-pahl	Principal – main. Plat – plate, dish. Main dish, main course.	Main course	
Purée (f)	pooh-ray	Puréed material is blended, smoothed, like mash	Mashed potato	
Morceau (m)	more-soh	A **morse**l is a piece of something. A tasty morsel.	Piece (bit)	
Tartine (f)	taahr-teen	**Tart** makes us think of food. Tart**ing** up your slice of bread by putting butter on it.	Piece of bread and butter	
Pizza (f)	peets-ah		Pizza	
Recette (f)	reuh-sett	**Reci**pe and **rec**ette are quite similar	Recipe	
Reçu (m)	reuh-sooh	The proof of payment is **rec**eived by the client. Reçu means received.	Receipt	
Satisfait(s)/ satisfaite(s)	sah-teese-fay/sah-teese-fet	**Satisf**ied	Satisfied	
Menu (m)	meuh-noo	This is something of a false friend, menu meaning a **set** menu.	Set menu	
Tranche (f)	trawsh	In the First World War soldiers sliced up the ground, making **tre**nch**e**s	Slice	

Word or phrase	Pronunciation guide	Aide-mémoire	English meaning	Check
Spécialité (f)	spay-see-al-ee-tay		Speciality	
Entrée (f)	awn-tray	Entrance in to the meal occasion	Starter	
Hors d'œuvre (m)	oar-deuhv-reuh	Means **o**ut**s**ide (h**or**s d') the w**or**k of art (œuv**re**). Not the main attraction.	Starter	
Bifteck (m)	beef-tek	A mixture of beef and steak, **bif te**ck	Steak	
Sucreries (fpl)	sook-reuh-ree	**Su**ga**ries**	Sweet things	
Soif (f)	swaaff	Qu**aff** a **swi**g to quench thirst. In French, 'I have thirst', 'j'ai soif' means 'I'm thirsty'.	Thirsty	
Pourboire (m)	pouhr-bwaahr	P**our** – f**or**. **B**oire – to drink (**b**everag**e**). Money **for** the server **to** have a **drink**.	Tip	
Plateau (m)	plah-toh	A 'plateau' is a high but **flat** piece of land, like a tray. A **plat**ter is like a tray.	Tray	
Serveur (m)	sair-veuhr	A server of food	Waiter	
Serveuse (f)	sair-veuhze	A serveuse of food. Feminine ending like mass-euse.	Waitress	

Practise!

List the five most difficult words to remember from this list. Justify why you think they are difficult.

1. _____

Reason: _____

2. _____

Reason: _____

3. _____

Reason: _____

4. _____

Reason: _____

5. _____

Reason: _____

25: Le corps
[The body]

Word or phrase	Pronunciation guide	Aide-mémoire	English meaning	Check
Cheville (f)	sheuh-vee-yeuh	Anklle. **Ch**é sprained his ankle in a **vill**age.	Ankle	
Bras (m)	brah	You must move your bras to put on your bra, a **bra**celet goes round the arm.	Arm	
Dos (m)	doh	If you are **dos**sing about, you are lying around, on your back, le dos	Back	
Bide (m)	beed	Starting letter is the same. I 'bide' off more than I can chew! Not!	Belly	
Vessie (f)	vess-ee	**N**essie doesn't need to worry about her vessie (bladder), living in Lough Ness	Bladder	
Fesses (fpl)	fess	Fesses rhymes with mess. I've got nothing else, scraping the bottom of the barrel.	Bottom	
Seins (mpl)	sah	Parisian ladies might go skinny-dipping in the **Sein**e!	Breasts	
Cerveau (m)	sair-voh	**Cer**ebral activity is brain activity	Brain	
Mollet (m)	mawl-ay	My cow has a calf named 'Mollay'	Calf	
Coude (f)	kouhd	Coude you point me in the right direction, using your elbow?	Elbow	
Doigt (m)	dwah	**Dig**its, for p**oin**ting	Finger	
Pied (m)	pee-yeah	Pedestrian, podiatrist, pied – foot	Foot	
Cheveux (mpl)	sheuh-veuh	Read this in an English accent: "If it's cold you shiver and your hair stands on end." Shiver sounds like cheveux.	Hair	
Main (f)	mah	You **man**ipulate with your hand	Hand	
Tête (f)	tet	Tête à tête (head to head) in English describes a meeting between just two people. **Tet**ty bears have heads.	Head	
Cœur (m)	cair	**Car**diac, **cor**e of an apple	Heart	
Talon (m)	tah-law	The talon of an eagle is found on its heel	Heel	
Hanche (f)	awe-sheuh	Starting letter the same. I have a 'hanche' you won't forget it, it's so hip!	Hip	
Reins (mpl)	rah	**Ren**al	Kidney	
Genou (m)	zheuh-nouh	**Genu**flexing is an English term which means to bend your knees	Knee	
Jambe (f)	zhawm-beuh	You get a leg of h**am**, if you are **jam**my	Leg	
Foie (m)	fwah	When you realise the importance of the liver, you just stand back and say, 'Fwah!'	Liver	
Poumons (mpl)	pouh-maw	Pulmonary organs	Lungs	
Nombril (m)	nawm-breel	Start and end letters are the same. Ombre – shadow. The contents of an 'inny' are in shadow.	Navel	

Word or phrase	Pronunciation guide	Aide-mémoire	English meaning	Check
Cou (m)	couh	**Co**llar is your neck	Neck	
Tibia (m)	tee-bee-yah	Same, biologically	Shin bone	
Épaules (fpl)	ay-pohl	É denotes 's' which is the same starting letter. Épaulettes are decorative shoulder pieces.	Shoulder	
Peau (f)	poh	Your skin **pee**ls in the sun. And it is mostly water, p**eau**. **Eau** is water.	Skin	
Crâne (m)	krahn	Your **cran**ium is your skull	Skull	
Plante (f) des pieds	plawnt-day pee-yeah	Plant your foot down – you plant the sole of your foot on the ground	Sole	
Ventre (m)	vawn-treuh	Do you have the stomach for the ad**vent**ure?	Stomach	
Estomac (m)	ess-stom-mah	Looks like 'stomach' – apart from that E, which you could eat, thereby putting it in your stomac!	Stomach	
Cuisse (f)	kweese	Repeat this phrase: "The geese have incweesed the size of their thighs."	Thigh	
Gorge (f)	gorrh-zheuh	A gorge is a deep valley, where a river runs, which is like the throat, when we drink	Throat	
Pouce (m)	pouhss	Think of Pouce in Boots with Tom Thumb	Thumb	
Doigts (mpl) de pied	dwah deuh pee-yeah	Digits of pedestrian (they use their feet)	Toe	
Orteil (m)	ohr-tay	Got the letters of toe – **orte**il	Toe	
Taille (f)	tye-yeuh	**Tail**ors measure around the waist	Waist	
Poignet (m)	pwahn-yay	The handle of a frying pwahn-yay is like a wrist before the pan, which is the hand	Wrist	

Practise!

1. Draw up two lists of five body parts, in French. In one list, you will put what you regard as the five most important parts of the body. In the other you will put your five least important parts of the body.

The most important five
(les cinq les plus importants)

The least important five
(les cinq les moins importants)

_____   _____

_____   _____

_____   _____

_____   _____

_____   _____

2. Determine which parts of the body are being described in each of the following.

Je l'utilise (I use it) pour penser _____

Je les utilise (I use them) pour respirer _____

Je l'utilise pour protéger (protect) mon cerveau   C ___ ___ ___ E

Je l'utilise pour faire le signe d'au revoir   _____

On utilise une brosse pour brosser les   C ___ ___ ___ ___ ___ X

Ici, on digère ce qu'on a mangé   E ___ ___ ___ ___ ___ C

En France on mange les   C ___ ___ ___ ___ ___ S de grenouille

3. What do each of the following mean? Three have been done for you.

J'ai mal aux bras	I have sore arms
J'ai mal à la tête	_____
J'ai mal aux jambes	_____
J'ai mal au cou	_____
Je me suis fait mal à la tête	I have hurt my head
Je me suis fait mal à la jambe	_____
Tu t'es fait mal au bras	_____
Il s'est fait mal au dos	_____
Je me suis cassé le poignet	I broke my wrist
Tu t'es cassé la main	_____
Elle s'est cassé la hanche	_____
Elle m'a brisé le coeur	_____

26: Les parties de la figure
[Parts of the face]

Word or phrase	Pronunciation guide	Aide-mémoire	English meaning	Check
Joues (f)	jouh	Jowels are cheeks on an animal	Cheek	
Menton (m)	mawn-taw	**Men** can have **ton**s of chins. Don't **ment**ion the chins!	Chin	
Oreille (m)	oar-ay-yeuh	Oral and aural ability depend on your ears	Ear	
Oeil (m)	ay	**O**cular (**o**eil) is to do with the eye	Eye	
Sourcils (mpl)	sourh-seal	These are **sur** (above) the lashes	Eyebrow	
Cils (mpl)	seal	Cilla, the name, is almost a combination of **Cil** and **la**sh. Cilla has lashes of lashes.	Eyelash	
Paupières (fpl)	poh-pee-yair	You **peer** by opening your eyelid. They cover your **pee**pers.	Eyelid	
Les Yeux (mpl)	lays-yeuh	At least it has the **ye** of **ey**es – 'les' tells us it is plural	Eyes	
Figure (f)	fee-goohr	Her face cuts a fine figure	Face	
Visage (m)	vee-zah-zheuh	His face is a **vis**ion. En**visage** – to turn your face to something.	Face	
Front (m)	fraw	The **front** of your head is your forehead	Forehead	
Gencive (f)	zhaw-seehv	**Genciv**itis is gum disease and the starting letter is the same	Gums	
Mâchoire (f)	mash-wire	Papier mâché is chewed paper. You use your jaw to chew.	Jaw	
Lèvres (fpl)	lehv-reuh	Starting letter is the same. The **levers** of your mouth.	Lips	
Bouche (f)	bouh-sheuh	'Fermez la bouche' – shut your mouth. A **bu**t**che**r provides for your mouth.	Mouth	
Nez (m)	nay	Similar	Nose	
Dents (fpl)	daw	**Dent**ist	Teeth	
Rides (fpl)	reed	Little beasties could **ride** along your wrinkles in their little cars	Wrinkle	

Practise!

Draw a face, and
label it appropriately,
in French.

27: Les maladies, les conditions et les médicaments
[Illnesses, conditions and medicines]

Word or phrase	Pronunciation guide	Aide-mémoire	English meaning	Check
Après-soleil (m)	ah-pray soh-lay	Soleil, solar, to do with the sun. Après – after, e.g. après-ski, après-midi, après-soleil.	After-sun lotion	
Antibiotiques (fpl)	awn-tee-bee-ot-eek		Antibiotics	
Bombe (f) antiseptique	prod-wee awn-tee-sep-teek	Antiseptique is a giveaway. A bombe explodes with particles of spray.	Antiseptic spray	
Asthme (m)	asth-meuh		Asthma	
Jambe (f) cassée	zhawmb cassay	You get a leg of h**am**, if you are **jam**my. Cassée – cracked, broken.	Broken leg	
Varicelle (f)	vah-ree-sell	The 'very cells' go red and itchy	Chicken pox	
Rhume (m)	room	When you have it, you have no **rh**o**om** in your nose for anything, it's blocked!	Cold	
Compression (f) cérébrale	cawm-press-yaw say-ray-brahl	Compressed is pressurised with a bang. Cerebral – to do with brain.	Concussion	
Toux (f)	touh	Toux, **to**nsil, throat, cough	Cough	
Sirop (m) pour la toux	see-roh pore la touh	Syrup	Cough syrup	
Croûte (f)	crouht	û denotes an 's' after the u. Crust is linked to scab.	Crust, scab	
Égratignure (f)	ay-grat-een-yoohr	é denotes 's' at the start of a word. Here a **s**crape, **s**cratch. Grat > grate > graze.	Cut (graze)	
Pansement (m)	paw-seuh-maw	Prance about wearing a dress....ing	Dressing	
Goutte-à-goutte (m)	gouht-ah-gouht	Rain **drip**s into the **g**o**utte**r	Drip	
Drogue (f)	drog		Drug	
Eczéma (m)	ek-zay-mah		Eczema	
Premiers soins (mpl)	preuh-mee-ay swah	Premier league, first league, first care, aid	First aid	
Fièvre (f)	fee-ev-reuh	Fever	Fiver	
Grippe (f)	greep	In the **grip** of the flu	Flu	
Être enrhumé(e/s)	et-reuh aw-room-ay	When you have it, you have no **rh**o**om** in your nose for anything, it's blocked!	Have a cold	
Ça ne va pas	sah neuh vah pah	Means it is not going. I am not going well.	I'm not well	
Aux urgences (fpl)	oh zoor-zhawse	In the place where **urgen**t cases go	In A&E	
Indigestion (f)	ah-dee-zhest-yaw		Indigestion	
Inhalateur (m)	een-ahl-at-euhr		Inhaler	
Peau (f) qui me gratte	poh kee meuh grat	Peau – **pe**el, skin. Gratte – grate, scrape, scratch, itch.	Itchy skin	

Word or phrase	Pronunciation guide	Aide-mémoire	English meaning	Check
Boîter (v)	bwah-tay	Boîte – a box. If your leg joint comes out of its box, you will limp.	Limp	
Rougéole (f)	rouh-zhay-ole	Rouge – red. Red spots are measles.	Measles	
Médecine (f)	made-seen		Medicine, the profession	
Médicaments (mpl)	may-dee-kah-maw	**Médic**aments	Medecines	
Oreillons (mpl)	oh-ray-yaw	To do with your oreilles (ears). Link to aural, which is to do with listening and hearing.	Mumps	
Pommade (f)	paw-mad	Pummel, massage, rub in ointment	Ointment	
Plaie (f) ouverte	play ouh-vert	Open is overt, and you can get cut while **plaie**-ing	Open wound	
Doliprane (m)	doll-ee-pran	Doli – linked to dolor – pain. Prane is linked to pain.	Paracetamol	
Comprimé (m)	kawm-pree-may	**Compre**ssed powder is a pill	Pill, tablet	
Sparadrap (m)	spah-rah-drah	A drape is a cover, so is a plaster, 'drape it over'	Plaster	
Plâtre (m)	plat-reuh	â denotes an 's' after the a, pl**as**ter	Plaster cast	
Enceinte(s)	awe-saahnt	Enceinte ends in an 'e' because it describes a woman. **Enc**los**e**d in the mum.	Pregnant	
Ordonnance (f)	oar-dawn-awnse	An **ord**er made for a patient	Prescription	
Remède (m)	reuh-med	Remedy or cure	Remedy	
Rubéole (f)	roo-bay-ole	Looks like and is also called German Measles	Rubella	
Cicatrice (f)	see-kah-treese	Ci**catr**ice, scar	Scar	
Frissons (m)	free-saw	Fridge, freezing, shiver	Shivers	
Malade	mah-lad	**Mal** denotes illness, badness	Sick	
Maladie (f)	mah-lad-ee	**Mal** denotes illness, badness. -ie is generally the ending of a noun.	Sickness	
Somnifère (m)	sawm-nee-fair	In**somni**a is not sleeping	Sleeping pill	
Écharpe (f)	ay-sharp	É denotes 's' at the start of a word. A sling is like a scarf (**sch**a**r**pe).	Sling	
Mal (m) au bras	mahl oh brah	**Mal** is a prefix meaning 'bad' or sore. Bras is arm. No **h**arm in a bra – actually there is!	Sore arm	
Mal (m) à la gorge	mahl ah lah gore-zheuh	**Mal** is a prefix meaning 'bad' or sore. Gorge is a big chasm down which water flows.	Sore throat	
Mal (m) aux dents	mahl oh daw	**Mal** is a prefix meaning 'bad' or sore. Dentist, teeth.	Sore teeth	
Pastille (f) pour la gorge	pass-teel pore lah gor-zheuh	A gorge is a passage that water runs down, like a throat. Pastilles are pastilles.	Sore throat pastille	
Entorse (f)	aw-torse (like gorse)	Torse is like tearing which is like spraining	Sprain	
Piqûre (f) de moustique	pee-koohr deuh mouh-steek	**Pri**cked, stung	Sting of a mosquito	
Point (m) de suture	pwah deuh soo-toohr	Sutures are stitches, stitch points	Stitch	

Word or phrase	Pronunciation guide	Aide-mémoire	English meaning	Check
Coup (m) de soleil	kouh deuh soh-lay	If you cowp, you fall over. **SOL**ar burning can knock you over.	Sunburn	
Insolation (f)	ah-soh-lass-yaw	In**sol**ation. The **sol**ar effect. Insulation is about heat.	Sunstroke	
Angine (f)	aw-zheen	Angina is heart disease. A sore throat is not so dangerous, but it is an ailment.	Throat infection	
Fatigué(e/s)	fah-tee-gay	Fatigue is tiredness	Tired	
Se faire arracher une dent	seuh fair ah-rash-ay oon daw	Ah-rash-ay, sounds like ripping something out, leaving a gash…ay.	To get a tooth removed	
Se faire suturer (v)	seuh fair soo-too-ray	Make oneself sutured, i.e. get sutured	To get stitches	
Se faire soigner (v)	seuh fair swaan-yay	Get treated medically, soigner, linked to sanitary, conditions in hospital	To get treated	
Se faire maltraiter (v)	seuh fair mal-tret-ay	Mal – malice – bad	To get treated badly	
Aller chez le médecin	all-ay shay leuh may-deuh-sah	Aller, **go** down an alley. Médecin provides medicine. Chez Bill. Chez le médecin (Doc's).	To go to the doctor	
Échographie (f)	ake-oh-grah-fee	**Sound echo**es allow a **graph** or picture to be created	Ultrasound	
Radio (f)	rah-dee-oh	Radioactive waves created the X-ray	X-ray	

Practise!

Some illnesses and conditions are listed below. Find the appropriate remedy and write it beside the given condition. Or, if you are given the remedy, find the condition.

La condition	**Le remède/traitement**
1. une toux	_____
2. une jambe cassée	_____
3. _____	une écharpe
4. mal à la gorge	_____
5. mal aux dents	_____
6. une égratignure	_____
7. _____	une écographie
8. _____	des antibitoiques
9. la varicelle	_____
10. un coup de soleil	_____

28: Les pays, les endroits
(Countries, places)

Word or phrase	Pronunciation guide	Aide-mémoire/Example of usage	English meaning	Check
Afrique (f)	ah-freek	Je vais en Afrique	Africa	
Australie (f)	oh-strah-lee	Tu vas en Australie	Australia	
Autriche (f)	oh-treesh	Il va en Autriche (to see an ostrich)	Austria	
Belgique (f)	bel-zheek	Elle va en Belgique	Belgium	
Brésil (m)	bray-zeel	Elle va **au** Brésil	Brasil	
Bulgarie (f)	bool-gahr-ee	Nous allons en Bulgarie	Bulgaria	
Canada (m)	kah-nah-dah	Vous allez **au** Canada	Canada	
Chine (f)	sheen	Ils vont en Chine	China	
Croatie (f)	kroh-ass-ee	On va en Croatie	Croatia	
Chypre (f)	sheep-reuh	Elles vont en Chypre	Cyprus	
République (f) tchèque	ray-poo-bleek chek	Je vais en République tchèque	Czech Republic	
Danemark (m)	dan-maahrk	Je vais **au** Danemark	Denmark	
Angleterre (m)	awn-gleuh-tair	Anglo-saxon is an old term for E**ngl**ish. Je vais en Angleterre.	England	
Estonie (f)	ess-tohn-ee	Tu vas en Estonie	Estonia	
France (f)	fross	Elles vont en France	France	
Finlande (f)	fah-lawnd	Il va en Finlande	Finland	
Allemagne	aahl-man-yeuh	Ger**ma**gn, Alle**magn**e. Elle va en Allemagne.	Germany	
Grèce (f)	gress	Nous allons en Grèce	Greece	
Hollande (f)	all-awnd	Vous allez en Hollande	Holland	
Hongrie (f)	awn-gree	Ils vont en Hongrie	Hungary	
Inde (f)	and	Elles vont en Inde	India	
Irlande	ear-lawned	On va en Irlande	Ireland	
Japon (m)	zhah-paw	Je vais **au** Japon	Japan	
Léttonie (f)	lay-tohn-ee	Tu vas en **Lét**tonie	Latvia	
Lithuanie (f)	lee-too-ahn-ee	Il va en Lithuanie	Lithuania	
Luxembourg (m)	looks-awm-bouhr	Elle va **au** Luxembourg	Luxembourg	
Malte (f)	maahlt	Nous allons en Malte	Malta	
Mexique (f)	meks-eek	Nous allons en Mexique	Mexico	
Irlande du Nord	Ear-lawned dooh norrh	Vous allez en Irlande du Nord	Northern Ireland	
Les Pays Bas	payee-bah	Low, bass countries. **Pa**ys, (**pa**triot) where the sea can flood in. Ils vont **aux** Pays Bas.	Netherlands	
Pologne (f)	poh-lawn-yeuh	Elles vont en Pologne	Poland	
Portugal (m)	por-too-gaahl	On va **au** Portugal	Portugal	
Écosse (f)	ay-koss	É replaces 's' – therefore **Scot**s. Tu vas en Écosse.	Scotland	
Slovaquie (f)	sloh-vah-kee	Tu vas en Slovaquie	Slovakia	

Word or phrase	Pronunciation guide	Aide-mémoire/Example of usage	English meaning	Check
Slovénie (f)	sloh-vay-nee	Il va en Slovénie	Slovenia	
Espagne	ess-pahn-yeuh	E**spagn**e. Nous allons en Espagne.	Spain	
Suisse (f)	sweese	A Swiss is from Switzerland. On va en Suisse. Ils vont en Suisse.	Switzerland	
Suède (f)	swed	A Swede is from Sweden. Je vais en Suède.	Sweden	
Royaume (m) Uni	roy-yohm-ooh-nee	Uni, united. Royaume is the (aume, ome, home) of the roy, king (royal). Il va **au** Royaume Uni.	UK	
États Unis (mpl)	ay-tazz-ooh-nee	É denotes 's', therefore states. Unis – is united. Elle va **aux** États Unis.	USA	
Pays de Galles (m)	payee-deuh-gahl	W**ales**. Nous allons **au** pays de G**alles**.	Wales	

Practise!

Write down 3 lists, without gaps.

- List 1: Countries that border Pologne. Start with 'Pologne', e.g. Polognelithuanie...
- List 2: Countries that border Serbie.
- List 3: Countries that border France.

You may find it helpful to consult the map of Europe below.

29: Les langues et les nationalités
(Languages and nationalities)

Word or phrase	Pronunciation guide	Aide-mémoire	English meaning	Check
Américain(s)/ américaine(s)	ah-mair-ee-kah/ ah-mair-ee-ken		American	
Autrichien(s)/ autrichienne(s)	oh-treesh-yeah/ oh-treesh-yen		Austrian	
Belge(s)	bell-zheuh		Belgian	
Britannique(s)	bree-tah-neek		British	
Candaien(s)/ canadienne(s)	kah-nah-dee-yeah/ kah-nah-dee-yen		Canadian	
Chinois/chinoise(s)	sheen-wah/sheen-wazz	Chinois relates to **Chin**ese	Chinese (nationality/ language)	
Citoyen(s)/citoyenne(s)	see-twy-yeah/see-twy-yen	**Cit**oy**en**	Citizens	
Anglais/anglaise(s)	awe-glay/awe-glezz	Anglais relates to **Engl**ish	English (nationality/ language)	
Européen(s)/ européenne(s)	ooh-roh-pay-yeah/ ooh-roh-pay-yen		European	
Étranger(s)/étrangère(s)	ay-traw-zhay/ay-traw-zhair	'é' replaces 's' at start of the word. Stranger means foreigner.	Foreign/ foreigner/ foreign woman	
Français/français(e/s)	fraw-say/fraw-says	Français relates to **Frenc**h	French (nationality/ language)	
Allemand(s)/ allemande(s)	ahl-maw/ahl-mawnd	If you remember the man of Ger**man**..., Allemand	German (nationality/ language)	
Indien(s)/indienne(s)	ahn-dee-yeah/ahn-dee-en		Indian	
Italien(s)/italienne(s)	ee-tah-lee-yeah/ ee-tah-lee-yen		Italian (nationality/ language)	
Japonais/japonaise(s)	zhah-poh-nay/ zhah-poh-nezz		Japanese (nationality/ language)	
Langue (f)	lawn-geuh	**Langu**age	Languages	
Écossais/écossaise(s)	ay-koh-say/ay-koh-sezz	É replaces 's' – therefore **Sco**ts	Scottish	
Langue (f) des signes	lawn-geuh day seen-yeuh	Langue – tongue or **langu**age. Signes – signs. Language of signs.	Sign Language	

Word or phrase	Pronunciation guide	Aide-mémoire	English meaning	Check
Espagnol(s)/ espagnole(s)	ess-pan-yawl/ess-pan-yawl	E**sp**agnol relates to **Span**ish	Spanish/ Spaniard (nationality/ language)	
Suisse(s)/suisesse(s)	sweese/sweese-ess	Suisse sounds like Swiss	Swiss	
Gallois/galloise(s)	gahl-wah/gahl-wazz	W**al**es, G**al**lo**is**. Little link. It's **gal**ling that so few speak Welsh.	Welsh (nationality/ language)	

Practise!

Pick out eight languages from the section above and pair them with the names of the countries where they originate. The first one has been done for you. Note that the names of the languages are masculine (le/l'), despite the fact that the word for language (la langue) is feminine.

Les langues   **Les pays**

1. L'anglais   Angleterre

2. _____   _____

3. _____   _____

4. _____   _____

5. _____   _____

6. _____   _____

7. _____   _____

8. _____   _____

…cances
…days)

…hrase	Pronunciation guide	Aide-mémoire	English meaning	Check
À l'étranger	ah lay traw-zhay	é replaces an 's', therefore 'stranger'. Stranger than home is abroad.	Abroad	
Aéroport (m)	ah-ay-roh-pore		Airport	
Dans un apartement	daws ahn ah-paar-teuh-maw		Apartment (in an)	
Chez moi	shay-mwah	Chez moi – at my home. Chez nous – at our home. 'Shay' it, then take it home.	At my home	
Au bord de la mer	oh boar deuh lah mair	On the **bord**er of the **mer**maid place, the sea	At the sea-side	
Bâteau (m)	bah-toh	Battre – to beat, the water – eau. **B**e**at**s the water.	Boat	
Vacances (fpl) actives	vah-kaws ak-teehv	A **vaca**tion is a holiday	Busy holidays	
Camping-car (m)	cawm-ping-kaahr	It's a camping car, not a van!	Camper van	
Camping (m)	cawm-ping		Camping	
Caravane (f)	caravan		Caravan	
Cathédrale (f)	kat-ay-draahl		Cathedral	
Bon marché	baw-mar-shay	Good – bon. Markets – marché are cheap. Note: 'ils sont bon marché' – 'they're cheap'.	Cheap	
Peu cher(s), chère(s)	peuh shair	Peu – linked to petit, a little. Little expensive (not expensive), cher, cherished, dear.	Cheap	
Froid(e/s)	frwah (frwahd)	Fridge	Cold	
Confortable	caw-for-tah-bleuh	Don't be co**nn**ed by the **n**	Comfortable	
Pays (m)	pay-ee	**Pa**triotic is pride in country	Country	
À la campagne (f)	ah lah kawm-pan-yeuh	We go **camp**ing in the countryside	Countryside (in the)	
Culturel(le/s)	cool-toohr-ell		Cultural	
Est (m)	esst		East	
Cher(s), chère(s)	shair (both pronounced this way)	If you **cher**ish someone, you hold them dear, dear is expensive	Expensive	
Ferry (m)	fair-ee		Ferry	
Premier(ère/s)	prem-ee-yay (prem-ee-yair)	First league, premier league	First	
Hôtel (m) cinq étoiles	oh-tel sank ay-twaahl	In étoile, the é denotes 's', like **st**ar	Five star hotel	
Étranger(s) (étrangère/s)	ay-traw-zhay, (ay-traw-zhair)	É replaces 's', which would make 'stranger' which is linked to foreign	Foreign	
Quinzaine (f)	kah-zen	-aine attached to a number means 'approximately'. Quinze+aine is literally 'approximately 15' but means two weeks.	Two weeks/ fortnight	

Word or phrase	Pronunciation guide	Aide-mémoire	English meaning	Check
Complet(s) (complète/s)	cawm-play (cawm-plet)	**Complet**ed jigsaw puzzle is one that is finished, full of pieces	Full (no vacancies)	
Visite (f) guidée	vee-zeet gee-day		Guided tour	
Port (m)	pore	Port, harbour same thing	Harbour	
Serviable(s)	sair-vee-ah-bleuh	**Serv**ing is helping	Helpful	
Voiture (f) de location	vwah-toohr deuh loh-kass-yaw	**Vi**a means road. Cars go via roads. When in another **location** you hire.	Hire car	
Location (f)	loh-kass-yaw	It's the right occasion, we're in the right location. Let's hire bikes!	Hire/rental	
Gite (m)	zheet	'We went on holiday to France and stayed in a Git!'	Holiday cottage	
Vacances (fpl)	day vah-kawss	**Vaca**ti**ons**	Holidays	
Chaud(e/s)	show (shode)	**Ca**lor gas is gas for heat. A **chau**ffeur heats his boss' car up before driving it.	Hot	
Hôtel (m)	oh-tel		Hotel	
Impoli(e/s)	ahm-poh-lee	**Poli**te, and the im- making it the opposite	Impolite, rude	
Clef/clé (f)	klay	A treble clef is a musical indication of the key to the music	Key	
Sympathique(s), sympa	sam-pat-eek, sam-pah	**Sympatheti**c to one's needs means that one is kind	Kind	
Dernier(ère/s)	dair-nee-yay (dair-nee-yair)	Comes from de retro (of past), retrospective, looking back	Last	
Petite virée (f)	peuh-teet vee-ray	If you **veer** off somewhere, it is a little trip	Little trip	
Hôtel (m) bas de gamme	oh-tel bah deuh gaahm	Bas, **bas**s note, low note. Gamme, the whole **gam**ut, range, low end of range.	Low cost hotel	
Hôtel (m) de luxe	oh-tel deuh looks		Luxury hotel	
Mois (m)	mwah	**Mo**nth	Month	
Monument (m)	maw-noo-maw		Monument	
À la montagne (f)	ah lah mawn-tan-yeuh		Mountains (in the)	
Prochain(e/s)	prosh-ah (prosh-en)	Ap**proach** means to move beside, the one beside is the next one	Next	
Nord (m)	norrh		North	
À la côte (f)	ah lah coat	The 'ô' denotes 's' after 'o', like coast	On the coast (sea)	
Au bord (m) de la mer	oh bohr deuh lah mair	The **bord**er is the edge, the coast. A maid in the mer, a mer-maid in the sea.	On the seaside	
Outre-mer	ouh-treuh mair	Outraged really means over-raged, so 'outr-' is 'over'. Mer, mermaid, sea.	Overseas	
Lieu (m)	lee-yeuh	'In lieu' of in English means in **place** of. '**Lieu**tenant'. Tenant responsible for place.	Place	
Endroit (m)	awn-drwah	On **D**r**wad**, on his shoulders, that's the **place** to be!	Place	

Word or phrase	Pronunciation guide	Aide-mémoire	English meaning	Check
Argent (m) de poche	ar-zhaw deuh posh	**Ar**gent is silver, chemical symbol, **Ag**. Silver of **pou**che, or **poc**ket.	Pocket money	
Piscine (f) municipale	pee-seen mooh-nee-see-pahl	Piscine is unfortunately what can happen in them. Municipal, means 'of town'.	Public swimming pool	
Raisonnable(s)	ray-zawn-ah-bleuh	**R**ai**sonnable**	Reasonable, good value	
Région (f)	ray-zhee-yaw		Region	
Billet (m) aller-retour	bee-yeah al-ay reuh-touhr	Billet – pay a dollar **bill** for your tick**et**. Aller – alley – go down an alley and return.	Return ticket	
Château (m) de sable	shah-toh deuh sah-bleuh	â denotes 's' after the 'a', makes it closer to **c**ha**st**le, **sa**ble and **sa**nd	Sand castle	
Seine (f)	sen	Literally, you must be '**in Seine**' if you bathe in it	Seine (Paris river)	
Vacances (fpl) de ski	vah-kawss deuh skee		Ski holidays	
Sud (m)	sood		South	
Spectaculaire(s)	spec-tak-ooh-lair		Spectacular	
Séjour (m)	say-zhouhr	A sojourn is a stay. Jour (meaning 'day') is hidden in séjour. Spend few days, stay.	Stay	
Stressant(e/s)	stress-awe, (stress-awnt)	**Stress**ant	Stressful	
Grandes vacances (fpl)	grawnd vah-kawss	Vacation	Summer holidays	
Vacances (fpl) d'été	vah-kawss day-tay	The accents in 'été' are like droplets of sweat	Summer holidays	
Crème (f) solaire	krem soh-lair	**Solar** cream is sun cream	Sunscreen	
Nager (v)	nah-zhay	**Na**vy, **na**utical, to do with the water	Swim	
Tente (f)	tawnt		Tent	
Tourisme (m)	touh-reez-meuh		Tourism	
Bâteau (m) mouche	bah-toh mouhsh	Battre – to beat, the water – eau. The boat is like a fly (mouche) zipping about Paris.	Tourist river boat (in Paris)	
En ville (f)	aw veal	Ville, village – but actually a town/city	Town/city (in)	
Inattendu(e/s)	een-ah-tawn-doo	Attendre – the verb to wait (you expect service from a waiter). In- = un-expected.	Unexpected	
Villa (f)	vee-lah		Villa	
Semaine (f)	seuh-men	**Se**ven days in a week	Week	
Ouest (m)	ouh-esst		West	
Vacances (fpl) d'hiver	vah-kawss dee-vair	Hiver – winter. **Hi**b**er**nate.	Winter holidays	
Monde (m)	mawnd	A **mo****und** of Earth that is our world	World	
Auberge (f) de jeunesse	oh-bair-zheuh deuh zheuh-ness	Jeunesse – juvenile, junior, youth. Auberge – Where do young **auberg**ines hang out?	Youth hostel	

Practise!

1. Here is a passage on holidays with a few missing words. The missing words are given below, in English, in a random order. Find what these missing words are in French and then fill them in to the blanks.

Town/city	sea	south	caravan	to swim	tourist boat
campsite	beside the sea	hot	cold	monuments	Seine

L'année dernière, je suis allé dans le _____ de la France dans ma

_____. Nous sommes restés dans un _____

près de la mer Méditerranéenne. C'était super parce que j'étais _____

donc j'ai pu _____ chaque jour dans la _____.

Quand on y était il a fait _____ et j'ai adoré ça. Je préfère avoir chaud

que d'avoir _____. L'année prochaine, nous allons retourner en France

mais cette fois-ci, nous allons aller dans une grande _____ qui s'appelle

Paris. C'est la capitale de la France. Je pense que ça va être super parce que je vais pouvoir visiter les

_____ comme l'Arc de Triomphe et la tour Eiffel et aussi, on va pouvoir faire

une excursion sur la rivière qui s'appelle la _____. Cette excursion sera en

_____ et je vais pouvoir voir Paris la nuit.

2. Translate the following holiday story into English.

L'année dernière, je suis allé dans le nord de la France près de Calais au bord de la mer. Je suis allé en ferry de Belfast en Écosse et puis en voiture dans le sud de l'Angleterre. Nous avons pris le ferry de Douvres à Calais et nous sommes allés directement au camping qui était à 5 kilomètres du port de Calais. C'était bien pendant trois jours mais après trois jours il a commencé à faire froid et on n'a pas pu nager dans la mer. Nous sommes allés à la piscine municipale mais il y avait trop de personnes et ce n'était pas bien. En fait, les vacances ont été un peu stressantes!

_____

_____

_____

_____

_____

_____

_____

31: La mer, l'eau douce
[The sea and fresh water]   [Not on the CCEA core vocabulary list]

Word or phrase	Pronunciation guide	Aide-mémoire	English meaning	Check
Plage (f)	plah-zheuh	Plage and beach have a similar sound, the same number of letters, and there is an 'a' and an 'e' in both.	Beach	
Cabillaud (m)	kah-bee-yoh	**C**abillau**d**, **c**o**d**	Cod	
Crabe (f)	crab		Crab	
Crustacé (f)	crooh-stah-say		Crustacean	
Poisson (m)	pwah-saw	**P**i**sce**s, zodiac fish sign. **P**os**e**idon was the Greek god of the sea, **Pes**catarian.	Fish	
Pêche (f)	pesh	**P**i**sce**s, zodiac fish sign. **P**os**e**idon was the Greek god of the sea, **Pes**catarian.	Fishing	
Eau (f) douce	oh-douhss	Eau, three vowels run together like running water, aqua. **Dul**cet tones are sweet tones, fresh water is sweeter than salt water.	Fresh water	
Langoustine (f)	law-gouh-steen		Langoustine	
Homard (m)	oh-maarh	Bart served one up to 'Homard' Simpson	Lobster	
Sirène (f)	see-ren	Siren, a sea nymph, a mermaid who lures sailors to death by singing (siren sound)	Mermaid	
Moule (m)	mouhl		Mussel	
Huitre (m)	weet-reuh	Remember, the 'h' is not pronounced, so hui**tre** sounds a bit like oys**ter**	Oyster	
Crevette (f)	crev-ett	A **cr**ustacean which looks like the **cr**awfish, its frenchwater cousin	Prawn	
Rocher (m)	roh-shay	**Roc**her and **roc**k	Rock	
Voilier (m)	vwah-lee-yay	A veil is a piece of cloth, like a sail – there's the link, veil, **voil**ier	Sailing boat	
Marin (m)	mah-rah	Marine, a sea soldier, sub-marine, under sea	Sailor	
Saumon (m)	soh-maw		Salmon	
Sable (m)	sah-bleuh	**Sa**nd and **sa**ble linked	Sand	
Coquille (f) St Jacques	coh-kee-yeuh sah zhack	Cockle (coquille) is a shellfish, like a scallop. St. John (St Jacques) is often depicted wearing a scallop shell round his neck.	Scallop	
Mer (f)	mair	A maid from the sea is a **mer**maid	Sea	
Fruits (mpl) de mer	frwee deuh mair	Fruits of the sea. Mermaid – sea maid.	Seafood	
Algues (fpl)	aal-geuh	Algae is a green water-based plant like seaweed	Seaweed	
Requin (m)	reuh-kah	**In** – from **f**in – a **requi**em mass will be **requi**red if one of these **fin**ishes you off	Shark	
Pierre (f)	pee-yair	**Pie**rre and **pe**bble linked	Stone, pebble	
Truite (f)	tr-weet		Trout	
Thon (m)	taw	The tuna wears scampi (skimpy) clothing. In fact this animal favours the **thon**g!	Tuna	
Vague (f)	vah-geuh	**Va**gue and **wav**e are linked. Also linked to **ve**nt, **ve**ntilate, **w**ind.	Wave	
Baleine (m)	bah-len	As big as a **bal**loon is the balubbery wh**ale**	Whale	